PLANES, STEAK & WATER

Title: Planes, Steak, & Water
Subtitle: Defending Donald J. Trump
Copyright © 2016, Autry J. Pruitt. All Rights Reserved.

Requests For Permission To Make Copies Of Any Part Of The Work Should Be Submitted To:
Urrepublic Productions
Attn: Planes, Steak & Water
7600 Chevy Chase Drive – Suite 300
Austin, TX 78731
books@urrepublic.com

Editor: Sheldon

Autry J. Pruitt, Autrypruitt.com

Printed in the United States of America
First Printing: September 2016

Hardcover ISBN: 9781619845558
Paperback ISBN: 9781619845565
Ebook ISBN: 9781619845572
LCCN: 2016952936

Library of Congress Record: https://lccn.loc.gov/2016952936

PLANES

STEAK &

WATER

DEFENDING DONALD J. TRUMP

AUTRY J. PRUITT

CONTENTS

I am always & forever grateful.

This work is formally dedicated to Emma, Audrey, Leonid, Margarita, Larisa, and Lovelynn.

If they put Donald Trump in,
try to put him in office, if that's what
the people want, you are going to see
an end to the Republican Party.
It will just be over, there'll
just be nothing left.

—MEGYN KELLY, *The Kelly File*, December 16, 2015

CHAPTER 1

"A CHANGE IS GONNA COME"

THE YOUNG SINGER stepped up to the microphone, inhaled the smoky atmosphere, and gazed out over the crowd. The stage lights caught the faint glistening of sweat below his hairline. It was the early sixties in Harlem, and the packed venue wasn't air-conditioned. People furiously fanned themselves with whatever they had on hand. The singer could make out a few familiar faces, some black and some white. All were there for the same reason—to see a gospel artist sing a pop song.

"He's already legendary," someone toward the front whispered, and that made the handsome man on stage bite his lip to stifle a smile.

He grabbed the microphone, listened for his lead-in, and let his powerful, smoky voice work its magic. The mesmerized audience leaned forward on their barstools.

From the start, everywhere this man went, his following grew. The church stage became the local club, which in turn led to larger venues and then television appearances. His voice— somehow smooth and edgy, vulnerable and manly at the same time—soon led fans and critics alike to crown him the "King of Soul." Although it was the height of the Civil Rights Movement, Sam Cooke seemed to show nothing but promise.

In late 1963, after finishing a set at a local nightspot, Sam Cooke and his band strolled into the Holiday Inn of Shreveport,

Louisiana. They approached the front desk and made no effort to tone down their laughter or to stifle their boisterous attitude. It had been a great night, and they were going to enjoy it. One of them smiled and nodded to the night auditors at the front desk before giving their names.

Instead of the fawning reception to which the band had grown accustomed, they were met with blank stares from the hotel clerks. A shadow fell over Cooke and his band as each of them realized what was happening. They were being turned away. The people behind the counter didn't know who Sam Cooke was and, frankly, didn't care. They didn't rent rooms to blacks, and that policy was not going to change.

Cooke lost his cool. He went off on the people at the front desk and refused to budge. His wife, Barbara, stepped in and with a gentle touch of his arm said, "Sam, we'd better get out of here. They're going to kill you."

"They're not going to kill me! I'm *Sam Cooke!*"

He held his head proudly, chin up, until Barbara whispered, "No, to them you're just another 'you know.'"

A month or two after the incident, Sam wrote "A Change Is Gonna Come," the composition of which, he later said, came easier to him than any other song had. His lyrics were an example of the patience his people had to have while waiting for change:

"It's been a long time, a long time coming
But I know a change gonna come, oh yes it will."

The bridge of the song reminds us just how difficult change can sometimes be:

"Then I go to my brother
And I say brother help me please
But he winds up knockin' me
Back down on my knees, oh."

Cook didn't rely upon oblique references and esoteric metaphors when crafting the lyrics to "A Change Is Gonna Come." The message about bigotry and discrimination was plain, stark, and powerful. This is perhaps why the song has transcended the civil rights era and remained potent and vital even in today's world. On the 50th anniversary of the song's release, Bill Flanagan of VH1 noted the following: "It adapts to changing circumstances while remaining constant. It promises progress while admitting that progress comes slowly and with great sacrifice."

The message of this song may as well have been written for the Republican Party.

REPUBLICAN PARTY 1861-2015

The Republican Party has long been known as the GOP, an abbreviation that stands for Grand Old Party. It was born in the 1850s out of the disaffected former members of the Whig and Free Soil parties. Founded as an abolitionist party, the Republicans have gone through myriad incarnations over the years, because in politics, as in life, change is inevitable. Yet the question remains: How much change can the GOP accept before it no longer recognizes itself?

Even more to the point, was the nomination of Donald J. Trump necessary for the party to remain viable?

For most of their history, the Republicans have been focused on the preservation of the United States as a nation, which meant reminding voters of our constitutional values. They revered Thomas Jefferson (even though he and other Founding Fathers despised all political parties) and worked to limit the size and scope of the federal government, while enabling states to determine their own path. Over the decades, they faced serious opposition from the

Democrats, who were never as intent on preserving national unity as they were on expanding government and increasing the size of the social safety net. The Republicans traditionally viewed themselves as the group that anchored us to our founders' ideals.

However, somewhere along the way, the Republicans started to lose their focus. Instead of attempting to preserve the United States according to its founding principles, the party began to attempt to preserve the status of its party elders and party seats. The apparatus slowly became infested with apparatchiks, party hacks, men without chests—the type of uninspired boors who make statements such as *remember to go along to get along* and *don't upset the apple cart* and *wait your turn, young man*. It became a party of old men who had forgotten why they were there.

To many observers, the official death knell for the party occurred on June 26, 2015—the day the United States Supreme Court legalized gay marriage. If ever there was an epitaph to be chiseled on the tombstone of the Republican Party, it is the words of Justice Anthony Kennedy, who wrote: "[Homosexuals'] hope is not to be condemned to live in loneliness, excluded from one of civilization's oldest institutions. They ask for equal dignity in the eyes of the law. The Constitution grants them that right."

This monumental decision brought a number of responses from Republican Party standard-bearers. Former Louisiana governor Bobby Jindal summed it up for the old-guard, noting that "marriage between a man and a woman was established by God, and no earthly court can alter that." These reactions were, for some Republicans, a gross over-exaggeration, but for many party traditionalists, heartfelt. Many Republicans fretted for the nation's very soul, concerned that tomorrow's America would resemble yesterday's Sodom and Gomorrah. Other, perhaps more strategically adept, party members were more pragmatic, asking themselves important questions about identity.

The problem: few mainstream Republicans offered any solutions that bridged the divide. Granted, this was a Supreme Court decision, but it was also the culmination of many years of political neglect. The ruling was especially hard to accept because social conservatism was the only plank remaining in the party, since fiscal restraint had flown out the window almost 35 years earlier.

Let's look at that in plainer terms. To protect our founding American ideals, the Republican Party has historically championed all policies that benefit the family—and that includes any policy that helps families keep more of their own money. Thus, Republicans have always demanded fiscal restraint on the part of the government. Under this model, both money and power should be kept as close to the family as possible. As the distance from the family grows—to local government, then state government, then finally to federal government—the power government's institutions have over families should drastically decrease.

For Republicans, a country that is deep in debt and that commits itself to foreign obligations ultimately will erode the family. This is because both will raise taxes upon the common people, reducing the family's ability to support itself. In this scenario, eventually the family will cease to rely on itself and will instead become reliant upon the government. At that point, the family unit will break down. Some would argue this is the case now.

This is the foundational reason behind the GOP's traditional belief in fiscal restraint. The principle of balanced bookkeeping tells us that the government should spend only the money that it takes in annually, through taxes, and not a dollar more. Ideally, the budget would be balanced each and every fiscal year—and, certainly, no corporate bailouts.

This idea was usually yoked to some associated planks, including low taxes, free trade, and privatization of government services. In a 2011 *MarketWatch* article titled "Four Things Republicans

Used to Be," writer Rex Nutting noted that Republicans used to value low tax rates while recognizing that some taxation is necessary and good. The old Republican philosophy, he says, was to raise the revenues needed by the government with the expectation that the government wouldn't spend money if it didn't need to. David Burton, an economist at the Heritage Foundation, noted that it's hard to call yourself a conservative if the free market gets all the profits, and the taxpayer gets all the losses. This position has been supported with varying degrees of success by many major thinkers across the decades, from Friedrich von Hayek to William F. Buckley, Jr. to Milton Friedman and his economics department at the University of Chicago.

WHAT HAPPENED TO FISCAL RESTRAINT?

Fiscal restraint is still followed at local levels (mostly), but at the federal level, it began a slow march toward death with bailouts during the reign of Richard M. Nixon. Ironically, it was the following decade that saw the putative ascendancy of Republican philosophy, epitomized by the presidency of Ronald Reagan. He became the touchstone forever after for all subsequent Republican politicians, who invoke his name like a holy grail. *Reaganesque* even became an adjective used to describe a politician who was friendly, beloved, on message, and seemingly made of Teflon.

But did the eight years of Tip O'Neil (Democratic Speaker of the House) and Ronald Reagan really represent a glorious period of fiscal restraint? No.

The reason: during and after Reagan's presidency, the GOP decided to throw fiscal conservatism out the window. They had inflated the national debt to nearly biblical proportions in an effort to outspend the Soviet empire on defense. Later, the administration of George W. Bush pursued two wars—in ret-rospect, one just and one unjust—and put the bill for both of them on our future, cutting taxes on the wealthy at the same time. Anyone with basic experience in accounting can tell you this is poor financial planning, but that is exactly what our Republican-led government did in the early 2000s. Bush's administration alone inflated the national debt to $9 trillion. Eight years earlier, when he took office, there had been a surplus of more than $100 billion.

Of course, this sort of betrayal had also occurred before Reagan. Richard Nixon used federal funds to bail out Lockheed Martin in 1971. A few years later, President Gerald Ford did the same for Franklin National Bank. The savings and loan debacle saw Reagan sticking his hand into the federal pocket, not to defeat communism, but to defeat the idea that the federal government wouldn't rush to the rescue of drunken gamblers on Wall Street. (It would, and still does.)

Such bailouts grew even more frequent, and by 2008, the economy had entered one of the periodic crises that characterize market economies, but this one was more severe than most. Treasury Secretary Henry Paulson convinced Congress to pass the Emergency Economic Stabilization Act, with the provision that the Treasury Department would buy $700 billion worth of troubled mortgages from the banks and modify them to help struggling homeowners, which was on top of a secret emergency Federal Reserve bailout of at least $9 trillion. Such a promise brought in skeptical Democratic lawmakers, who then agreed to pass it. Days later, the Federal Reserve and the Treasury decided to abandon the plan in favor of direct injections of billions in cash to companies such as Goldman Sachs and Citigroup. This was known as the Troubled Asset Relief Program (TARP), and it was accomplished with borrowed money.

As a result, without a fiscal leg to stand on, the GOP was left with little choice but to turn to their other core belief—social conservatism. They had to overemphasize these social issues because no one was buying their fiscal conservative shtick. Instead, they hammered away on anti-abortion measures and anti-contraception measures since both are important to the party's deeply religious faction, the basis of the family. They attacked prostitution, which as the world's oldest profession, isn't exactly a front-burner issue, and proudly announced their support for law and order, particularly in continuing the ineffective war on drugs. In early 2016, they took aim at North Carolina's transgender bathroom law, which is about as peripheral as an issue can be.

They had to take odd steps to ensure that their base continued voting for their up-ballot candidates. This meant making sure that there was always an anti-abortion measure on as many state ballots as possible. They had to get the people into the voting booth to pull a straight-Republican lever, even if the voters didn't care much for the increasingly globalist candidates who were being continuously floated as presidential candidates, including both Bushes, Bob Dole, John McCain, and especially Mitt Romney. The party came to rely heavily upon churches to prop them up because they capitulated in policy to Democrats, regardless of who was president, on issues ranging from NAFTA to No Child Left Behind to Medicare Prescription D. To keep that constituency solidified, the Republicans bent over backward to show evangelical associations just how pious they could be, and a certain background in Protestant churches became a necessary part of a candidate's curriculum vitae. Over time, the Republican constituency morphed into a strange alliance between global elites, religious conservatives, and ordinary businesspeople acutely aware of the bottom line.

Of course, it was never a perfect union, and the cracks in that alliance had been showing all along, judging by the party's weak reactions to events. Republicans used to believe in a strong presidency in times of war, especially when it came to foreign affairs. In fact, the Bush administration saw an increase in presidential power and use of unilateral authority. However, when Democratic President Barack Obama ordered a no-fly zone over Libya, something both parties wanted, Republicans still reacted angrily. In other words, they liked an unquestioned commander in chief when it was a Republican, but a Democratic president was, in their eyes, unqualified to make the same type of presidential decisions.

Furthermore, Republicans had been quite vociferous for many decades about the primacy of the states over the power of the federal government. This cry of states' rights, of course, has been taken up by both parties—the Democrats during Andrew Jackson's era—but the Republicans have been the loudest. Nowhere is this tension clearer than in the battle over health-care reform.

The fact is, Republicans used to believe in universal health coverage. In the 1970s, President Richard Nixon offered a health-care plan to Congress that looked a lot like the 2010 Affordable Care Act (ACA)—better known as Obamacare—but Teddy Kennedy rejected it for not being liberal enough. Later, while governor of the state of Massachusetts, uber-Republican Mitt Romney signed a state law creating a precursor to the ACA. It was proof that universal health care could have been accomplished at the state level, which is in keeping with classic Republican values, but the Republicans didn't ever achieve this or even push for it. Instead, Barack Obama and the Democrats got the federal government involved, which contradicts the Republicans' view of such matters.

It's no wonder Sam Cooke's song comes to mind. A change *had* to come. *Went to my brothers, said brother help me please, but he ended up knocking me on my knees.* If you were a good Republican voter, you went to your brother during the 2010 and 2014 midterms and gave the GOP both houses of Congress. At the state level, you went to the ballot box and delivered to the GOP 74 percent of all governors' mansions. At the local level, you probably voted in as many Tea Partiers as you possibly could since the Tea Party was a largely evangelical reaction to this strange drift that the party had been taking. If you lived in Virginia in 2014, you may have even played a role in the biggest congressional upset of all time, the election of David Brat (total campaign donations: $200,000) over sitting House Majority Leader Eric Cantor (total campaign donations: more than $5 million). If there was ever a David versus Goliath moment in congressional politics, that was it. You probably felt elated.

You don't feel quite so high anymore, do you? I'm willing to bet it feels more like you've been knocked down and crushed beneath an elephant's foot.

What did you get for diligently following the GOP and carrying out your right to vote? You watched as your party, especially at the federal level, took care of everyone else *except you.* You watched as your party studied, planned, and approved of a massive expansion of a police state via technology. You watched as your party abandoned smart political strategizing in favor of willful obstructionism. In the words of Robert Kagen of *The Washington Post*:

> the repeated threats to shut down the government over policy and legislative disagreements, the persistent calls for nullification of Supreme Court decisions, the insistence that compromise was betrayal, the internal coups

against party leaders who refused to join the general demolition— [these things] taught Republican voters that government, institutions, political traditions, party leadership and even parties themselves were things to be overthrown, evaded, ignored, insulted, laughed at.

In 2005, in a feeble attempt to get back into your good graces, your party offered up to you the unholy triumvirate of Jeb Bush, Ted Cruz, and Marco Rubio for the office of the presidency. Bush's last name alone put an awful taste in your mouth—his brother having left office with some of the lowest approval ratings among Republicans in history, the country mired in debt, and his presidency considered a disaster by analysts on both sides of the aisle. Ted Cruz was a supposed constitutionalist who, you learned, solicited money in the form of loans from Goldman Sachs and Citibank, an arrangement that was certainly never part of the Constitution. Marco Rubio conveniently forgot where his family came from and decided to try his hand at legalizing illegal immigration before being slapped down by other U.S. senators.

Your party also gave you John Roberts, the new chief justice of the Supreme Court, an ostensible Republican who in June 2012 made the controversial decision (twice) to uphold certain provisions of Obamacare—in full opposition to the principles of the Constitution. That was the second-to-last cord holding the Republican Party to its point of view.

This is why the Supreme Court's decision was so devastating. Defending socially conservative policies was the only remaining filament that tied the Republican Party to its original principles, and it basically snapped on that fateful day that the institution of marriage was extended to homosexuals. It was the straw that broke the elephant's back. It was (and maybe continues to be) diametrically and unambiguously opposed to Republican values.

Is it any wonder that the voters have finally erupted? Is it any wonder that the body politic, the common people, has shouted *enough*?

At last, we come back to the obituary: *After a long and courageous battle with its own core beliefs, America's beloved Grand Old Party, the party of Abraham Lincoln, passed from this earth on June 26, 2015.*

And when the Republican Party as we knew it died, the candidacy of Donald Trump was born.

Fairness is an across-the-board
requirement for all our interactions
with each other...Fairness treats
everybody the same.

—CONGRESSWOMAN BARBARA JORDAN

CHAPTER 2

ALL
THE PRESIDENT'S
WOMEN

ON A STAGE FULL of beautiful women, two were called to step forward. They faced one another and embraced, one with blond hair and a white dress, the other, black hair and a black dress. Both were striking; both were full of emotion as they awaited the next announcement.

"And the first runner-up is … Miss California!" The camera zoomed in on the astonished face of Miss Kentucky next to her, who put her hand over her mouth in shock. The crowd erupted in applause, and lights flickered on stage. Her name was Tara Conner, and the year was 2006. Grand bouquet in hand, Miss Kentucky was crowned Miss USA while she mouthed the words *thank you* to the crowd and judges.

Typically, Miss USA winners are paraded around the world as a role model for young women. However, with breathtaking speed, Conner dove into a lifestyle of drug abuse, alcohol abuse, and extreme sexual activities, all of which were impossible to hide from the public, particularly with the rise of social media. The *New York Daily News* reported that same year that she was on the verge of losing her crown after testing positive for cocaine, making out in public with her friend, Miss Teen USA Katie Blair, and sneaking men into their Trump Place apartment.

Conner's fate as Miss USA fell to Donald Trump, owner of the Miss USA pageants from 1996 to 2015. Trump allowed Conner to keep her crown, with the stipulation that she enter a drug rehabilitation program. At a news conference, he explained his position by insisting that everyone deserves a second chance. Trump's brother Fred died of alcoholism in his 40s, an event that undoubtedly weighed heavily upon his mind.

The next morning, on the award-winning talk show *The View*, a panel of women discussed Trump's decision. Rosie O'Donnell criticized much more than his handling of the situation. After saying she didn't care for Trump, calling him a "snake-oil salesman," O'Donnell harped on Trump for his failed marriages, affairs, and the children left in the wake of various relationships. O'Donnell also referred disparagingly to Trump's filing for bankruptcy, not bothering to mention that the bankruptcies were filed on some of Trump's businesses as strategic moves, and not on him personally.

Trump's rebuttal was even more brutal than O'Donnell's comments. He told *People* magazine that Rosie O'Donnell was a "real loser" and that she would regret saying that he had ever gone bankrupt. "I'll most likely sue her for making those false statements and it will be fun," he said. "I look forward to taking lots of money from my nice, fat little Rosie."

The feud continued over Twitter and through various media outlets for several years, with one nasty comment following another. On *Entertainment Tonight*, Trump stated, "If I were running *The View*, I'd fire Rosie. I'd look her right in that fat, ugly face of hers and say, 'Rosie, you're fired.'" Following O'Donnell's departure from *The View* in February 2015, Trump stated he wasn't surprised that she failed. "I like the show a lot, but let's face it, Rosie is a loser."

It's undeniable that Trump is a counterpuncher—very good at returning a blow for a blow, a snark for a snark. Sometimes it seems as if he has a ledger in which he keeps track of everything everyone has ever said about him. It's important to remember, though, as his life is being relentlessly analyzed during his campaign for the president, that his attitude toward women is no different than his attitude toward men. He's an equal opportunity verbal pugilist. In his way, Trump is a more practical feminist than most of the analysts who decry his treatment of women.

Case in point: Beginning at the Republican presidential candidate debate in August 2015, it seemed that Trump had found a new woman with whom to feud: Fox News host Megyn Kelly. During that debate, after hitting other candidates with a few edgy questions, the anchor turned both barrels on Trump.

"Mr. Trump," said Kelly, "one of the things people love about you is you speak your mind, and you don't use a politician's filter. However, that is not without its downsides, in particular, when it comes to women. You've called women you don't like 'fat pigs,' 'dogs,' 'slobs,' and 'disgusting animals.'"

Trump did not apologize for his comments. Instead, he said, "What I say is what I say. And honestly, Megyn, if you don't like it, I'm sorry." Applause erupted for both Kelly and Trump after this exchange—and a new feud was born. Trump doesn't take those sorts of frontal attacks sitting down.

When the debate ended, Trump tweeted that Megyn Kelly "really bombed tonight." He later added during a call-in interview with CNN: "She gets out and she starts asking me all sorts of ridiculous questions. You could see there was blood coming out of her eyes, blood coming out of her wherever." Trump insisted he was referring to Kelly's nose, while others interpreted his words as comments on her menstrual cycle.

After the debate and subsequent cantankerous news coverage, the two seemed to keep their emotions at bay. This truce of sorts was codified with a hastily arranged special interview on May 17, 2016—a surprisingly cordial event in which both parties shook hands and made nice. For his part, Trump admitted that debate was the first time he realized he could actually be President of the United States. He told Kelly he felt stung by her question: "When I am wounded, I go after people hard, Okay? And I try and un-wound myself."

This type of Trumpian reaction is nothing new—and definitely not limited to women. In 2013, *The Hollywood Reporter* posted a slideshow titled *Donald Trump vs. Everyone: His 20 Best Media Feuds*. Three of the 20 Trump feuds were not against specific people, but instead whole groups: *Deadspin* editors, *Salon*, and *Vanity Fair*. Of the 17 remaining feuds that Trump waged, 35 percent were with women and 65 percent were with men.

Is Trump nasty to women? Yes, absolutely. However, he's also nasty to men—and insults almost twice as many men as women.

Take for example his banter with billionaire and *Shark Tank* star Mark Cuban. In 2012, Cuban tweeted that he would donate $1 million to charity if Donald Trump shaved his head. Funny and harmless, right? Not according to Trump: "Offer me real money and I'd consider it. Your team and networks have lost so much money I doubt you have much left!" This year, Cuban has endorsed Hillary Clinton for president.

That wasn't the only time Trump counterpunched hard, no matter the reputation of the opponent. In 2011, Robert De Niro commented on Trump's search for President Obama's birth certificate: "It's like a big hustle; it's like being a car salesman." Soon after, on *Fox and Friends*, Trump responded. "I like his acting, but in terms of when I watch him doing interviews and various other things, we're not dealing with Albert Einstein."

Trump certainly has no problem insulting the outward appearance of men. He referred to Marco Rubio as "Little Marco" this past year in reference to the Florida senator's shorter stature (at least, one hopes). He commented that Nebraska Senator Ben Sasse, "looks more like a gym rat than a U.S. Senator." He has called Graydon Carter, the editor of *Vanity Fair*, "sloppy," "grubby," and a "total loser." *The New York Times* has assembled a list of every insult that Trump has ever made on Twitter, and both men and women are equal and fair game to Trump.

Gender isn't on Trump's radar. The bear doesn't care who is poking him. Man or woman, he's not going to tolerate it. Make no mistake about it, Donald Trump's comments to O'Donnell were vicious, but her comments toward him were equally horrible. Isn't it downright sexist to expect him to tread lightly with women who lash out at him, yet pivot to a no-holds-barred attitude toward men who criticize him? As corporate America moves ever closer to full gender equality, women should expect to be treated like men.

And men can be pretty brutal toward one another.

THE EVOLVING FACE OF SEXISM

The *Merriam Webster* dictionary defines *sexism* as "prejudice or discrimination based on sex; *especially*: discrimination against women." Traditionally, sexism is the belief that women should be confined to the home to care for their families. People of the Victorian era, for example, differentiated between the public and the private sphere; the former belonged to men and the latter belonged to women. Women were believed not fit to hold public positions and were seldom deemed suitable for leadership roles in any business environment.

Sexism is still present in American society today, and unfortunately, many people are oblivious to the fact that certain incidents or comments are discriminatory toward women. The difference today is that the modern workplace, depending on the industry, has far more female employees than ever before, and that includes the executive suites. Compared with the routine sexualization of women that was displayed in American offices prior to the sexual revolution—see *Mad Men* for an excellent example—the modern workplace has fewer instances of such overt sexism. Bosses today rarely refer to a woman as *sweetheart* or *sugar*, and rarely do they pat their secretaries on the rear end. This treatment kept a woman from having authority among her counterparts, and it is on its way toward being rightly eliminated. Women do face another, more insidious hurdle to overcome: intellectual sexism—the Hollywood perception that they bring with them social baggage that men won't. An employer may think twice about hiring a woman who is pregnant, or who already has children, because he or she assumes that the woman will need more time off than other candidates would. The employer may also assume, rightly or wrongly, that the woman will be too distracted. As a result, many women are then forced to choose between a family and a career. The problem is that not all women exhibit these types of presumed behaviors, and when they are presumed guilty before getting the job, it's a blatant form of sexism. Occasionally, as in the case of Melissa Nelson, a dental assistant who was fired by her boss for being too attractive, it can occur after being hired—in her case, long after (a decade, to be precise). Other women have resorted to dressing themselves down so that they can be taken more seriously.

Sure, things have changed, but women are still underrepresented in the executive suites of American businesses—that is, most American businesses. The offices of Donald Trump are the rare exception. In the early years of his career, Donald Trump often clashed with his father, Fred Trump, one of his most powerful influences, over this very topic. A real estate magnate in his own right, the elder Trump was a tireless workaholic who instilled in Donald the importance of passion for one's work. As a product of the first half of the 20th century, he also carried some of society's older prejudices about women in the workplace.

As the younger Trump began his rise in the world of Manhattan real estate, he found himself in a fundamental disagreement with his father: He wanted to hire women to work in construction. This might have been one of the first incidents in which Trump bumped up against the formidable will of his father on the job.

One of his most famous hires was Barbara Res. In 1980, Trump asked her to oversee construction of his now iconic Trump Tower. He called her "a killer," and used to comment that, "Men are better than women, but a good woman is better than ten men." In her book *All Alone on the 68th Floor*, she describes Fred Trump's thoughts on his son Donald hiring a woman to lead a construction project.

Fred did not like the idea that Donald had hired me. 'A woman?' Donald told me that. But I could tell by the way Fred treated me. He used to say that all the time: 'You don't know what you are talking about.' When I would complain to Donald about Fred, he would say, 'Fred didn't want me to hire you or didn't think it was a woman's job.'

Trump later mentioned to her that his father was from a different era and probably never would approve of a woman in such a position. But Donald Trump boldly went his own direction by placing women in powerful roles within his organization. As Ivanka Trump noted in her speech to the 2016 Republican National Convention, "There have always been men of all backgrounds and ethnicities on my father's job sites. And long before it was commonplace, you also saw women."

The reason for Trump's enlightened view of women in the workplace isn't altruistic. It isn't because he has a social justice crusader's vision, as some current CEOs seem to have. It's because he is acutely aware of the bottom line. He considers how much profit his companies can earn from his employees and his buildings, and he makes decisions based upon that. Years ago, Trump recognized that women were one of society's untapped resources and hired females to work in roles others didn't think they could handle. He valued their intelligence and their talent. Donald Trump is at heart a meritocrat, someone who believes in rewarding excellence, man or woman.

Today, Trump has chosen to surround himself with women such as Katrina Pearson, his communications consultant, and Omarosa Manigault, director of African-American outreach for his campaign. Rhona Graff is Trump's current assistant and senior vice president. She's worked with him for 25 years and had no interest in being interviewed for *The Washington Post* article that detailed the women who work for Trump. She did, however, send an email in which she described her position as stimulating, with every day being different. She described Trump as, "brilliant, insightful, funny, charismatic, and surprisingly down to earth."

Another current Trump employee is Deirdre Rosen, the vice president of human resources for the Trump Hotel Collection. After working for publicly owned companies for seven years, she said that working for the privately owned Trump organization was an adjustment—but in a positive way. The family-run company offers employees a significant amount of flexibility to spend time with their children. According to public statements by his female employees, this is extraordinarily popular. And, unlike many typical workplaces, when family time is taken, the employee is not subjected to disparaging looks or comments. Simply put, the policy is respected and embedded as a part of the Trump culture. This is hard evidence that the way Trump runs his companies—giving space to his female employees to have children and dedicate time to their private lives without fear of losing their jobs—is very forward-thinking, and not unlike attitudes expressed by Bernie Sanders or in European culture, which many among the beltway left revere so passionately.

Around 2010, Jill Martin joined the Trump Organization as assistant general counsel. Martin was often unsure of her abilities; when a case went before the U.S. Court of Appeals for the 9th Circuit, she assumed that a more experienced lawyer, most of whom were male, would argue the case. Instead, clearly impressed with her skill and acumen, Trump chose Martin. Since then, she has described Trump as someone who "encouraged her to grow." In her words: "He pushed me when I needed it."

The most interesting example of a female employee of the Trump Organization is Lynne Patton, who is vice president of the Eric Trump Foundation and senior assistant to Eric Trump, Ivanka Trump, and Donald Trump. She works with the president of the foundation to oversee all operations, volunteers, events, outreach, social media, vendors, and corporate partnerships. Patton's resume is as long as her arm, but for our purposes, the most relevant fact about her is that she is also a black woman.

In May of 2016, Patton created a YouTube video that detailed her experience working with the Trumps. As the daughter of a man who grew up in Birmingham, Alabama during the Civil Rights Movement, and who became one of the most established and respected doctors at Yale University, Patton could no longer stand by and watch so many accuse her boss of discrimination. In the video, she described the Trump family as generous, compassionate, and philanthropic.

She describes the Trumps as extremely loyal, even choking up when she describes the help that the Trumps extended to her during her darkest hours: "Like many Americans, I have struggled with substance abuse and addiction. The Trump family has stood by me through immensely difficult times without hesitation or concern for their own reputation by association." Most other workplaces would have seen this as a liability and found a reason to let Patton go. The Trump family stood by her. She concludes the video by rejecting any notion that she was "encouraged" to make the five-minute film. She simply states that "this is the right thing to do. For me, it was an easy decision—just like voting for my boss Donald J. Trump should be an easy decision for you." Just as he was there for Tara Conner, Trump was there for Patton when she went through a rough patch, offering her a second chance.

The question remains: Is it possible to have respect for women, support their careers, and treat them the way all humans desire to be treated—and yet still appreciate their beauty and delicately intricate qualities? Let's hope so.

It's also worth noting that Donald Trump has four grown children (Eric, Donald Jr., Tiffany, and Ivanka). His daughter Ivanka is currently the Executive Vice President of Development and Acquisitions at the Trump Organization. She's involved with all aspects of the company's real estate and hotel management initiatives. She has launched her own lifestyle brand, IvankaTrump.com. If Trump didn't believe women could be successful in business, why would he be so supportive of his daughter's business ventures? His two grown sons, Donald Jr. and Eric, are also capable, and Trump could have entrusted all business affairs to them—but he knew Ivanka was just as capable—perhaps even more so, and he has rewarded her based upon her skill and acumen.

In this discussion of Donald Trump's women, it's worth noting that Trump has been married three times. This by itself isn't unusual; according to the Pew Research Center, 40 percent of new marriages involve remarriage for at least one person. It's estimated that approximately 42 million Americans have been married more than once. Most people have no qualms about walking down the aisle a second time. In fact, 57 percent of Americans have done exactly that. According to census data from 2013, over 9 million Americans have been married three times or more. That's approximately 5.3 percent of the total married population. Another way to think of it is that one in every 20 married people has said "I do" at least three times.

Trump is no different. He was married to Ivana Zelnickova, a Czech immigrant, from 1977 to 1992. She is the mother of his three oldest children (Ivanka, Eric, and Donald Jr.). After a rancorous divorce, he was married to Marla Maples from 1993 to 1999, which produced daughter Tiffany. He married his current wife, Melania Knauss, in 2005, with whom he has one more child—Barron.

Multiple marriages are commonplace and certainly nothing to be frowned upon in today's society. Often, the third marriage is the most stable of them all. It is sometimes referred to as the professional marriage, often undertaken less for love (which is fleeting) and more for compatibility (which is more stable). The media, unfortunately, paints Trump's most recent marriage to Melania in a horrible light. Her career as a fashion model, replete with a few salacious nude photos, leads many to believe she is little more than a trophy wife. However, her performance during her speech at the Republican National Convention demonstrated that, like his Ivanka, Melania is also more than a pretty face. While some of the text appears to have been borrowed from Michelle Obama's prior speech, even casual observers understand that this was not intentional—the sentiment was her own. Vague language that uplifts people often sounds similar.

But the more common method of attack, at least from leftists, will be to shame Melania for not having a full-time job. They assume that, because she's chosen to stay home, to take care of their son Barron, to let her husband move forward—that she is somehow less of a woman. That's patently absurd. It's no objection at all. The sexual revolution existed to provide women with more options, not to tell them what to do with those options. This avenue of attack on Melania is meant for a singular purpose: to shame any women who might think about staying home with their family in the future—which, once again, brings us back to the core principle of the Republican Party: the protection and elevation of family as an organizing principle of society.

The president should be counted on to treat every citizen fairly, and Americans should be able to count on that person to speak the truth. Donald Trump should be judged by the substantive actions he has taken; he should be judged on his history of giving women opportunities that are rare in business sectors dominated by men (i.e., construction and gaming). It is a curious case, no doubt, Donald doesn't seem to talk the talk, but he definitely walks the walk.

Despite his purposeful and meaningful support of women in the workplace, some of his worst poll numbers come from women. In April 2016, Gallup found that 70 percent of women held an unfavorable view of the real estate mogul, compared with 58 percent of men. It's true that more women vote Democratic than Republican, but he still needs to woo them, because they will form a majority of the electorate in November. Since his opponent is a woman, it's even more crucial that these voters abandon their *perception* of his attitude toward women—and instead understand the *truth* of his attitude toward women.

One problem that some women have with Trump is his view on abortion. He's taken nearly every possible stance on abortion over the years. This reflects the anguish that many American citizens feel about the practice. It continues to be a wrenching and incredibly complex issue, and simple, pat answers elude any thoughtful person. He didn't make things any better when he stated that, should Roe v. Wade be overturned, women who have abortions would have to be punished. He was speaking to Chris Matthews at that time, who is experienced at baiting politicians. That doesn't excuse Trump's answer, but it does leave room for us to understand why he gave the answer he did. In his mind, if a law exists, and a person violates that law, consequences must exist—otherwise, what is the purpose of the law? This was a no-win situation. Although Trump could have been balancing myriad concerns in his mind (such as the hypocrisy of fratricide laws when put up against abortion), he was caught in a trap. Understandably, he later tried to clarify, and Katty Kay, noted lead anchor from BBC World News America, commented that sticking to that original statement, "would have made it very difficult for Mr. Trump to close his gap with women voters. Since single, suburban women will probably decide the outcome of this election, that is something Mr. Trump has to do to become president."

Social conservatives have been infuriated by his walk-back. To be fair, Trump waded into the swamp of the most dangerous political issue since 1977, and it's the type of swamp that very few candidates escape from unharmed. It seems that Trump had only two options: to come down on the hard-line side of pro-life, demanding punishment—or to come down hard on the side of pro-choice, keeping it always legal, in all cases. Philosophically, it's worth remembering that life is rarely black-and-white—and also that politics is the art of compromise.

Or should we say, the art of the deal.

You know who wins a lot of hearts because of her "dedication to women"? Hillary Clinton. And yet, there seems to be a great divide between her words and her actions. For example, Hillary speaks vehemently about fighting for women's rights in Saudi Arabia, a country ranked 145th of 158 by the U.N. Development Program's Gender Inequality Index, meaning it's one of the worst places on earth to be born female. Yet the Clinton Foundation routinely collects money from the Saudi government that blatantly contradicts her stated beliefs on women's rights. It's contradictory, and an issue the Trump campaign should focus on in upcoming debates.

There's more. Let's not relive the Monica Lewinsky scandal of 1998; we all remember that one. And let's not forget that Hillary Clinton chose to "stand by her man" throughout the allegations, press releases, court hearings, and lies. It's arguable that she stepped back from the situation, no doubt embarrassed and hurt on many levels, and considered which path would benefit her most.

Before the scandal broke, Hillary was described as strong, dishonest, and intelligent by the Pew Research Center's survey. Two years after Bill's confession, she was then called, "strong, intelligent, brave, loyal, and good." A whole new set of political doors opened up for Hillary because she made Bill sleep on the couch for a few months, though she eventually invited him back into her bedroom, so to speak.

If Monica Lewinsky had been the only blip on Bill Clinton's radar and Hillary had chosen to work through that and stay, that'd be one thing. But many women have claimed that Bill Clinton assaulted them, and it seems every time one of them attempts to come forward, the story is shouted down by the mainstream, typically "feminist," media.

It might have started with Eileen Wellstone when Bill Clinton was only 23 at Oxford University. Wellstone complained of being sexually assaulted and while Clinton admitted to the encounter, he said it was consensual. He ended up leaving Oxford a year after the incident without a degree. However, that was before Hillary, so let's jump to the incidents that directly affect our current presidential candidate.

In 1979, after being elected governor of Arkansas, Mr. Clinton began a 12-year affair with model Gennifer Flowers, who taped phone conversations she had with Clinton. In his 2004 autobiography, Mr. Clinton admitted to a sexual encounter, but said it only happened once in 1977.

The night before Mr. Clinton was elected president, Paula Jones, a state employee of Arkansas, was escorted to his room where Clinton crudely flashed himself and demanded oral sex. While Mr. Clinton still denies that this transgression ever happened, Jones received a cash settlement of $850,000.

The list goes on and can be explored in more detail in the Fox News article, "A Millennials' Guide to Bill Clinton's 20+ Sex Scandals." There are so many instances of Bill Clinton treating women poorly that even the most faithful followers of the former president have to step back and scratch their heads for a minute.

Hillary's current position on sexual assault is that she always stands with the victim. Her website quotes her as saying, "I want to send a message to every survivor of sexual assault: don't let anyone silence your voice. You have the right to be heard." Yet, when her husband was running for president, Hillary called all allegations against Bill "bimbo eruptions."

"Hillary Clinton is the enemy of American women," Paula Jones said. She was recently interviewed by Aaron Klein on his talk radio show and called Hillary a two-faced liar and demanded an apology.

Some of the most damning charges leveled at the Clintons came from a young female lawyer and a campaign volunteer named Juanita Broaddrick. Two years after the Clintons married, Mr. Clinton was elected Attorney General of Arkansas. Soon afterward, the young female lawyer claimed that he forced himself on her with violence. The following year, Broaddrick said Mr. Clinton raped her during his campaign for governor; the friend she was sharing a hotel room with that night confirmed her allegations, as did four other reliable witnesses.

On January 6, 2016, Broaddrick tweeted out:

"I was 35 years old when Bill Clinton, Ark. Attorney General raped me and Hillary tried to silence me. I am now 73…it never goes away."

In a sense, all these women were twice-victimized: first, by Bill's actions and second, by Hillary's retribution. Considering the number of cover-ups that Bill and Hillary Clinton have engineered, defending her actions seems entirely partisan and opportunistic.

Hillary Clinton's gender notwithstanding, Donald Trump's personal women's advocacy is at the very least on par with hers. Numerous media articles celebrate all the ways Hillary has helped women, but it seems faint praise indeed considering that she's also worked hard to silence many of those women who most needed a champion.

It's clear that the left's arguments pointing out Donald Trump's alleged sexism are purely political; otherwise, Bill Clinton would have been crucified as a sexist, and Hillary Clinton pilloried for attacking women who are victims. The arguments about Donald Trump being sexist are a broader part of the narrative that various news outlets attempt to create—if they can keep Republicans labeled as sexist overall, then they have achieved their goal. (After all, in many ways Trump is a novice at name-calling when compared with the left's skills at this.) We need to remember that when women cried out against the actions of Bill Clinton and the retributions of Hillary Clinton, the meek and apologetic response from the media was that his private sex and family life had nothing to do with his public service.

If voters choose not to vote for Trump because of his policies or his character, that is acceptable and reasonable. But if they choose not to vote for Trump based upon the notion that Hillary Clinton has fearlessly advocated for every woman she has encountered in her career, that is detached from reality and hardly the basis for sound decision-making come November.

Hollywood's propaganda war against Trump, not surprisingly, mirrors the vapidity and speciousness of DNC attacks on Trump's attitude toward women. The Democrats' attachment to the Hollywood establishment is the height of hypocrisy, for the simple reason that Hollywood continues to be one of the most sexist industries in America. Consider the recent release, *Straight Outta Compton*, which led one critic to point out that "institutionalized sexual and intimate partner violence against black women continues to be all but invisible in mainstream discourse." It was the prominent and successful rapper T.I. who also intimated that he could not vote for a woman as the leader of the free world. Imagine if Clint Eastwood, Ted Nugent, or any white actor proffered such vile and blatantly sexist comments. The Democratic Party's need for black votes means they will look the other way, no matter how breathtaking the transgression against what are supposed to their core values—as long as they garner votes.

Actresses are routinely harassed and bullied into doing whatever it takes to stay beautiful for as long as possible. And the old television guard is still mostly male. Just take a look at the major late-night hosts on television: John Oliver, Stephen Colbert, Trevor Noah, Seth Meyers, Jimmy Kimmel, and Jimmy Fallon. If these guys hold their seats as long as the men before them (i.e. Carson, Letterman, Stewart), we have at least another 20 years of male-dominated TV to go. Female directors find it difficult to thrive, and lower-level female employees often are paid less than their male counterparts and find their advancement frequently blocked. And the ill treatment starts early; Emma Watson of the Harry Potter franchise commented that she was "called bossy because [she] wanted to direct the plays…put on for [their] parents," but the boys were never called such. This lines up squarely with the opinions of Jennifer Lawrence and Meryl Streep. The ACLU has indicated that the federal government is investigating gender discrimination in the entertainment industry, that is, the feds may be going after some of the Democratic Party's most vocal and wealthy supporters.

Donald Trump's actions, though, speak more forcefully than the words of the Clintons or the dismal play-acting of PC Hollywood potentates. Throughout his storied career, Donald Trump has kicked open the door to his organization for women, and not just for those who may toil away as secretaries and assistants, but for those who have what it takes to manage and contribute on the highest levels. Hollywood may have little use for ambitious women, but Trump highly values them—just ask the women who work with him.

Pages 33 to 38 can be found
after page 44

the terrorism in our cities, threaten our very way of life. Any politician who does not grasp this danger is not fit to lead our country. Americans watching this address tonight have seen the recent images of violence in our streets and the chaos in our communities. Many have witnessed this violence personally; some have even been its victims. I have a message for all of you: the crime and violence that today afflicts our nation will soon come to an end. Beginning on January 20th, 2017, safety will be restored. The most basic duty of government is to defend the lives of its own citizens. Any government that fails to do so is a government unworthy to lead."

Trump's timing couldn't have been better, since the national headlines had been filled for weeks with stories about police attacks in places such as Dallas and Baton Rouge. Overall, violent crimes rose in 2016, for the first time in decades, which Trump perhaps sees as the beginning of a worrying trend.

In the United States, there is a clear party divide on attitudes about race. The right maintains that the left engages in identity politics—even race-baiting—in the quest for votes. The left believes that the right ignores realities about race, such as statistics concerning death penalty enforcement and the yawning wealth gap between black and white households.

Because of this divide, however, politicians on both sides tend to be either gun-shy or intellectually dishonest when addressing racial issues. This dishonesty causes knee-jerk reactions: the left believes that any policy put forth by conservatives that seemingly affects any racial group must, by definition, be prejudiced, whereas the right believes that any policy proposal from the left that affects a racial demographic is purely an attempt to buy votes.

Donald Trump was a non-entity in racial discourse in this country prior to 2015. However, because he entered the presidential race, and did so amidst this perceived racial divide and made the comments he did, he found himself shunted into the former slot. Because he addressed realities about people who have darker skin, he was portrayed by the left and many in the mainstream media as someone who could be a cross-burning member of the Ku Klux Klan, though in over 30 years in the spotlight he has never displayed any kind of overt racism.

The deeper question here is the issue of real racism, which is defined as *the belief that all members of each race possess characteristics or abilities specific to that race, especially so as to distinguish it as inferior or superior to another race or races.* Broken down further, this means that racism equates to prejudice, discrimination, or antagonism directed against someone of a different race based on the belief that one's own race is superior.

EVERYONE'S A LITTLE BIT RACIST

In February of 2015, James B. Comey, the director of the Federal Bureau of Investigation, gave a speech at Georgetown University in which he quoted the song, "Everyone's a Little Bit Racist," from the Tony Award-winning Broadway musical *Avenue Q.* Comey said, "Look around, and you will find no one's really colorblind. Maybe it's a fact we all should face: everyone makes judgments based on race."

The existence of such implicit *bias* (a term we will revisit shortly), or unconsciously making evaluations based on race, has been acknowledged for years. Comey's comment recognizes the fact that we're essentially all products of our personal experiences. These experiences, in turn, lead to bias in human decision-making. A person who grows up in a gated community in Brentwood, California, will necessarily carry a different set of decision-making mechanisms from a person who grew up in a public housing project in the North Bronx in New York City. This is *inherited bias*, and it's a part of life. However, that, in and of itself, does not constitute racism.

Just because a policy may have an effect upon a certain racial demographic doesn't necessarily mean it's a hateful policy. How can one judge the difference? When faced with a policy that has a racially biased effect on a large subset of people, a nonracist is open to altering or adjusting the policy if necessary. However, a person who refuses to address the issue and, potentially, replace the policy is a racist.

Real race-based hatred, also known as bigotry, although often manifested through written law and public policy, starts in the heart. It is taught within families, and reinforced by communities, both in real life and online (a casual perusal of Twitter or comment sections on any number of political blogs will provide more than enough anecdotal evidence). Hateful racism is intentional and evinces a core belief that one group is inferior to another. It's malicious. For example, from the 1930s to the early 1970s, the Federal Housing Administration, under a policy initiated by Democratic President Franklin D. Roosevelt, refused to back loans in black neighborhoods. The federal government had a policy of redlining, which meant that the administration would actually put a red line on a map and allow—essentially require, really—banks to discriminate on the basis of ethnic ancestry. This is quite different from inherited bias, and even though the line between them is thin and somewhat subjective, there is a "tell": a long pattern of negative behavior toward other races.

According to this definition, it's impossible to make the argument that Trump's intentions are bigoted. They are *biased*, but bias is not bigotry. Bias can be adjusted; bigotry is in the heart. The proof is simple. As his substantial interaction with Latinos, Muslims, their co-workers, neighbors, and friends has grown, Trump has become more educated about the link between illegal families and those that are in the U.S. legally. On the surface, this seems simple, but in reality, it is far more complicated. Even President George W. Bush, a member of a conservative establishment dynasty, tried to get his cohorts to understand that, with each passing year, the line between alien and legal immigrant would become blurred as the lives of the authorized residents or new citizens joined with illegal immigrants through marriage and births. But they, now to their chagrin, ignored the reality of immigration and killed the aforementioned Republican President's reform bill in the senate at the beginning of his term. Trump now faces this same battle; and, appropriately, Donald Trump has made necessary adjustments to his immigration policy. Adjustments aside, however, this does not mean his policies will ignore the stated traditional and conservative goal of placing America first—his policy will be biased toward Americans but not malignantly hateful.

The left could make an argument that his proposed policy regarding Muslims is too biased; however, many of Trump's naysayers understand that given the extremist attacks on our soil and, indeed, around the world (not to mention the numerous daily threats you can find throughout social media), that argument fails to hold up under scrutiny. Thus, they latch onto the easier argument. They conflate the two terms and want the voter to assume that a biased policy is always inherently racist. Regarding Latinos, Trump's bias, some of his more colorful statements notwithstanding, has nothing to do with pigmentation or even ethnic background. It is rooted in process. An immigrant either went through the legal process of immigration, or did not. Period.

The left also makes an extraordinary effort to portray Trump in a racist light when it comes to African-Americans, a charge that seems entirely made up out of whole cloth; in fact, it's the failure of the mainstream media to refute his opponent's frequent portrayal of Trump as some kind of white cracker racist that substantiates charges of liberal bias on their part.

Similarly, much has been made about Donald Trump's attempt to woo black voters as the 2016 presidential election moves into its final innings. Naturally, Democratic operatives and their lackeys at CNN and The Huffington Post and MSNBC have expressed outrage at Trump's overtures to the black community. How dare this "racist" outsider tell black voters that the Democratic Party has failed them on every level?

"What have you got to lose?" Trump asked African-Americans, a question the left failed to directly address, because how could they without damaging their own brand?

Trump's questions should go further, be even more direct (even for Trump): "Sure, the Democrats talk a good game, but what have they *actually done for you*? Are you better off than you were eight years ago? What did Carter or Clinton or Obama actually *do for you*?" (We might expand this to ask what these administrations have actually *done to* African-Americans.)

Any honest answers to these questions would shine a light on the shadowy truth: Democrats realize that they need not actually accomplish a damned thing for this critical voting bloc. Why should they? They get 80-90 percent of the black vote based on rhetoric alone, election after election. If the only thing some of us had to do to make a living was interview for a job and then never actually have to show up and *get something done* to get paid every week, how many of us would gleefully ride that gravy train into the sunset?

And here's another dark truth: When the Dems do take action, their policies not only fail to help, but actually *hurt* black communities.

Their actions are inevitably in the form of expanding government programs rather than creating real, economic, capitalist opportunities. Black communities that are entrenched in the welfare state, that are isolated in a socialist world, set quite apart economically and geographically from the world of free enterprise, will never reach their true potential, will never quite break free of slavery and Jim Crow. But they will, apparently, continue to vote for the party that keeps them pacified and in their place.

EVERYBODY PLAYS THE FOOL

The Democratic Party has played African-Americans for fools. The Democrats have taken every opportunity to crow that they are "for" African-Americans; yet, at every turn, when given a choice between allowing African-American communities to make decisions that increase their self-reliance and economic status or maintaining control over the communities, Democratic leaders have chosen control over self-reliance for these communities.

It's a simple matter to historically connect the Democratic Party to Jim Crow, the KKK, and other racist policies and organizations. However, without going back very far historically, you can look at the modern-day African-American condition and directly tie it to policies and prescriptions created by the Democratic Party—policies that are either wildly ill-conceived or designed to keep the black community in the needy victim column, rather than in the successful victor column.

Trump has been in a full-court press designed to snatch African-American support away from the Democratic Party on one principle alone: merit. In other words, the Democratic Party has not only failed African-Americans; it appears as if they have *tried* to fail.

When Mexico sends its people, they're not sending their best. They're not sending you. They're sending people that have lots of problems, and they're bringing those problems with [them]. They're bringing drugs. They're bringing crime. They're rapists. And some, I assume, are good people.

—DONALD J. TRUMP, *From His Presidential Announcement*

CHAPTER 3

"SOME ARE GOOD PEOPLE"

ON A SULTRY weekend evening in Mesa, Arizona, Emily Bonderer dolled up and went out to a bar with a couple of her friends. Later, one hand leaning on the pool table, she chatted up a young man from Mexico who'd bought her a drink. She kept the conversation going, but she found herself more attracted to the guy's handsome friend, who was quietly sitting on a barstool nearby, listening to the conversation, clearly too shy to chime in.

Bonderer waited for this man to show some interest. But he kept his distance, which intrigued her even more. About an hour later, Bonderer and her now-tipsy girlfriends decided to call it a night. She said her goodbyes and slipped out the door. When she was about a block away, Bonderer heard a whistle coming from the direction of the bar. She turned around and there was the handsome, silent man. She smiled and gave him the "come hither" finger wag, and he approached.

They've been together ever since.

Emily and Raymundo Cruz, whom she calls Gordo, were eventually married, but they didn't ride off into the sunset and live happily ever after. Before they met, Raymundo had broken a United States immigration law that resulted in a 9C ban. Specifically, he'd entered the U.S.A, stayed for longer than the year permitted by his visa, was deported, and then re-entered without permission. As a result, he would have to live in Mexico for 10 years before he could file a waiver asking to return again. With no other viable choice, the couple chose to live in Ciudad Juárez, a Mexican town across the border from El Paso, Texas. Raymundo worked in a local factory, while Emily commuted to her job in El Paso every day.

Emily marched in protest rallies, worked for immigration reform, and even spoke to her congressperson, but to no avail. She was forced to accept the fact that her husband had broken the law and would need to pay his dues, even though it didn't seem fair. He was a good, hardworking man who didn't break any other laws or cause trouble.

They moved across the border in 2010, at the height of the drug wars, during a time when Juárez had the highest murder rate of any city in the *world*. Emily started a blog called *The Real Housewife of Ciudad Juárez*, where she documented all that she and Raymundo had endured to stay together, including her reactions to the first dead body she saw in her neighborhood and the birth of her second child in El Paso, which she documented on FaceTime so that her husband could witness it from the other side of the border.

Were U.S. immigration laws put in place to keep a kind, hard-working man out of the delivery room for the birth of his child? Is Raymundo Cruz one of the "good people" Trump referred to in his comment? And, if he is one of the good ones, what sense does it make that he cannot cross the border, even for the birth of his son?

Also consider Larissa Martinez, a 2016 high school graduate. Martinez's mother, fleeing an alcoholic husband, had taken her and her sister to McKinney, Texas, where some of their relatives had legally settled. Once in the United States, her mother filed papers to become legal—but was told there was a 15-year waiting list. She was told the process might take less time because her relatives were already there, but there were no guarantees.

In the end, she, like so many others, simply overstayed her visa, like so many others, and lived an invisible life. Martinez enrolled at McKinney Boyd High School and was an exemplary student, climbing her way to class valedictorian. She even earned a full scholarship to Yale University, which is legally not prohibited from enrolling undocumented students.

During her graduation speech, Martinez found herself in the national spotlight: during her graduation speech, she confessed to being an illegal immigrant, and the resulting video went viral. She said she wanted to be honest about her residency status, even though the United States remains divided on the issue of undocumented aliens. She said she wanted to speak up and help protect other illegal immigrants.

Are these the illegals Donald Trump was talking about when he said he wanted to build a wall "higher and higher and higher"? Have not the Cruz family and Martinez family proven they should be permitted to stay in the United States? Are they not deserving?

In fact, yes, these are the "good people" about whom Trump spoke. When Trump rails about "law and order," it seems clear that he is addressing street crime, terrorism, and gross abuses of our immigration laws. There is little in Trump's past or in his rhetoric to suggest that he is a stickler for petty regulations or the bureaucratic mindset. And there is little in his past or rhetoric to support charges from the left—and from some of the right who have allowed themselves to get sucked into the left's extreme PC mindset—to suggest that there is anything bigoted or racist in Trump's desire for safe streets, protection from terrorism, and a secure border. Consider: Trump has been in the public eye for decades. Even the rabid "reporting" efforts of the

Washington Post have failed to turn up a single incident to justify the left's hate speech against Trump (because isn't calling someone who has never shown any inclination for these traits a "racist" and a "fascist" the ultimate hate speech?). In reality, Trump wants what most of the rest of us in the United States want, and is going about doing what it takes to get these things done in a practical and hate-*less* way; his recent overtures to the government of Mexico prove as much.

Donald Trump launched his presidential campaign in 2015 with a broadside against illegal immigration. The quotation that has largely defined his campaign, the one that graces the beginning of this chapter, has become one of his most infamous—the claim that Mexico is sending us the worst of their society—particularly rapists. Trump cut too wide a swath with those words, but it's clear that the Mexican government has a history of corruption, and a history of moving as many of its problems north of the border as it can get away with—and it's been getting away with quite a lot in recent years.

Later, Trump broadened this anti-immigrant stance by announcing in a March 2016 CNN interview with Anderson Cooper: "I think Islam hates us," he said, later adding, "We have to be very vigilant. We have to be very careful. And we can't allow people coming into this country who have this hatred of the United States."

His position, though some think severe, is rooted in his desire to protect Americans from those who would do us harm— namely, extremist Muslims. There are, of course, constitutional obstacles to this plan, but in this announcement, Trump's intent in making such incendiary statements is clear.

Trump's acceptance speech at the Republican National Convention echoed these themes: "Our convention occurs at a moment of crisis for our nation. The attacks on our police, and

These points may seem unconnected to Donald Trump, but there is a purpose here, a pattern that will demonstrate exactly why *Trump* should appeal to the black community.

1. Academia is linked to college athletic programs. Academia leans sharply to the left politically. Yet, when it comes to the issue of whether NCAA athletes should earn money from endorsements and such, most faculty professors and university administrators remain silent on the issue—or oppose the idea. Of course, not all of the athletes are African-American; however, some of the highest performers *are* African-American, and colleges still get to make loads of cash from these minority kids. Yes, they do throw them a couple of free cheeseburger meals and t-shirts and, yes, top athletes are often awarded scholarships (for a degree that may offer little economic return anyway, given the weak economy). If they get injured during competition, they may face long-term health issues—and risk losing their scholarships. In other words, big liberal elite institutions have no problem hoarding loads of colored poor kids into an arena (similar to Caesar Augustus) and forcing them to fight for the adoring spectatorship of other liberal elites. They just don't want these minority kids to derive any tangible economic benefit from their hard work.

2. Democrats seek to divide. No nation is perfect. America certainly isn't. And every citizen should fight to make their nation better. African-Americans are well within their rights to protest and, at times, should do so. However, the Democratic Party seeks to separate African-Americans from their rightful opportunities in this country by demonizing what it is to actually be American. And Trump's singular message is: "Hey, if a crazy guy from Queens can do all this, you can, too." He won't

offer a stipend for remaining a victim; instead, he will create inclusive economic opportunity that will, finally, help raise the economic standards of the black community. And maybe he'll even make Republicans out of many of you! African-American votes swung toward the Democratic side when JFK was elected, and since then, African-Americans have blindly supported the Democrats. Sadly, JFK has been dead for over half a century, and while many things have changed, one thing has not: Democrats continue to count on the black vote to swing presidential elections their way, regardless of whether they deliver positive economic results (they don't) or keep their promises (they don't) or offer viable, practical solutions (they don't). It's crazy to keep doing the same thing over and over again and expect different results. The Democrats have had their chances for decades now, and they have failed black America. It's time to try something new. What have you got to lose?

In order for us to solve problems related to race, we have to be willing to have an open dialogue about this thorny subject. It's challenging, and it makes us uncomfortable, but an open dialogue means that a person must be able to express feelings that may contain bias—we are all the sum of our experiences or those of our circle of friends and family. Real bigotry should not be tolerated in a modern society, but bias is natural, has always existed, and is sometimes a positive thing.

For example, if you have kids, you have a bias to feed your kids before your neighbor's kids—this bias does not mean you necessarily think your neighbors' kids are less valuable than yours or that they don't have a right to eat; it simply means your kids are your priority. In fact, most bias usually reflects a setting of priorities, particularly in politics. After all, politics is the system by which we determine how limited resources are allocated. At the root of politics in any country is a clear bias: that country's needs come first. If this were not the case, if resources were unlimited and politics unbiased, there would be no need for borders, separate currencies, or even separate governments. Our hope is that bias is not informed by bigotry. Remember, the difference between real bigotry and bias is that bigotry is in the heart and is almost impossible to change, whereas bias can be changed through friendships, statistics, facts, and debate (again, see Trump's moderation and moves on the immigration issues and/or his outreach to the African-American community). Unfortunately, because the mass media leans left, and because most colleges now are packed with professors who seem more interested in progressive "activism" than in teaching, and because it's an election year, your chance of finding a single media outlet that will distinguish between the two is slim. Even the Republicans have stopped trying to make the distinction— in truth, they hardly did so in the first place.

So when you consider the true essence of Trump's proposed policies—that our borders (southern border in particular) should not be a no-man's-land, that Muslim extremism is one of the greatest threats to peace and liberty in our time, and that it is the duty of the government to uphold the laws and protect its citizens—then you realize that his intentions are sound and admirable, not the stuff of ranting fascists, but the stuff that has shaped America during it most challenging times.

Being perfect is about being able to look your friends in the eye and know that you didn't let them down because you told them the truth.

—*Friday Night Lights*

CHAPTER 4

FULL CAVEMAN

DESPITE THEIR 2007 undefeated season—or perhaps largely because of it—the New England Patriots found themselves often hated by much of the football-loving public. (Perhaps there was also something about Bill Belichick's perpetual scowl and oversized sweatshirt that didn't sit well with the American public on Sundays.)

That year, the Super Bowl stage was set in Arizona with a matchup between the perfect-record Patriots and the roller-coaster-ride, 10–6 New York Giants. Many expected a bloodbath, with most of the blood flowing Giants blue and gray. The Giants had only begun to show signs of greatness in the last few games; thus, it was hard to imagine them emerging victorious against a powerhouse like the Patriots, even more so because the boys from Boston had legend-in-his-own-time quarterback Tom Brady at their core.

What followed was one of the greatest football games in history. The Giants managed to sack Tom Brady five times, leaving him with a 29/48 completion stat, which wasn't great, especially by his standards. By the fourth quarter, the Giants were leading 10–7, and the audience was biting their nails to the quick.

With 2:45 left, Tom Brady led an 80-yard touchdown drive that finished in a third-and-goal completion to Randy Moss for a touchdown. The score went to 14–10, Patriots. The Giants would have to score a touchdown to win the game. A field goal wouldn't cut it.

Eli Manning kept a cool head and systematically moved his team down the field. Manning threw to David Tyree, who made a leaping, one-handed catch, securing the football between his right hand and the crown of his helmet to gain 32 yards. With 35 seconds remaining, Manning lobbed the ball 13 yards into the end zone and the secure grip of Plaxico Burress, who took a few easy steps, then knelt down for a quick prayer. Against all odds, the Giants won the title, recording one of the biggest upsets in the history of sports—and one of the best Super Bowl games of all time.

For 30 straight years, according to the Harris poll, pro football has ranked as the most popular sport in America. In 2015, nearly 50 million Americans watched the AFC and NFC championship games. There's a reason people wake up at the crack of dawn on Sunday to paint their faces, drive to a stadium, grill hot dogs in a parking lot, and sport their favorite player's name on the back of a jersey. There's a reason that ESPN continues to be one of the most consistently profitable networks owned by the Walt Disney Company. Football is not only fun and entertaining; it's also *real*. The wear-and-tear that football takes on men's bodies and minds has caused major controversy over the past few years, yet there seems to be no sign that football's popularity is waning. The game has gritty physicality. It is real. It's in-your-face honest, critics be damned.

The game's authenticity mesmerizes the American public, and we are hungry for more—and this hunger is mirrored in modern politics.

Certainly, we rarely found that authenticity in politics until 2016. Unfortunately, when it comes to most American politicians, what you see is not what you get. Unlike football, where all of the play, beautiful and ugly, is exposed to the world, politicians have hidden agendas. Often, they'll say whatever they think will get the American public on board, true or false, and finding the real person under the makeup and message is nearly impossible.

In the past, the U.S. president was nothing more than a voice heard over the radio station, or later, the face on the television screen. There was no such thing as Twitter, Facebook, podcasts, or the constellation of media options that have begun to shine in the past decade. Away from the mainstream media, there weren't many chances to glimpse inside that person's life. A vision of perfect leadership was created, controlled, and presented to the American public, which largely consumed it without question.

Quite a few past presidents have had mouths on them, but it was customary to keep their outspokenness hidden from the public. For example, in 1951, President Harry Truman relieved then General of the Army Douglas MacArthur of his post after he ignored orders not to advance in Korea. To the press, Truman said,

> This was the most extraordinary statement for a military commander of the United Nations to issue on his own responsibility. It was an act totally disregarding all directives to abstain from any declarations on foreign policy. It was in open defiance of my orders as President and as Commander-in-Chief. This was a challenge to the authority of the President under the Constitution.

That sounds like a perfectly presidential response, doesn't it? But what he actually said behind closed doors was this: "I was ready to kick him into the North China Sea…I was never so put out in my life." Years later, in 1973, *Time* magazine reported Truman as having said, "I didn't fire him because he was a dumb son of a bitch, although he was, but that's not against the law for generals. It if it was, half to three-quarters of them would be in jail."

In the 1960s, President Lyndon B. Johnson had a heated discussion with Greek Ambassador Alexandros Matsas about Cyprus. In the president's words: "F—— your parliament and your constitution! America is an elephant. Cyprus is a flea. Greece is a flea. If these two fellows continue itching the elephant, they may just get whacked by the elephant's trunk, whacked good." *Whacked* is mobster language, not exactly what you'd expect from the most powerful man in the world.

President Richard Nixon taped every conversation conducted in the Oval Office and eventually incriminated himself by doing so. In 1973, he said,

The Jews have certain traits. The Irish have certain—for example, the Irish can't drink. The Italians, of course, just don't have their heads screwed on tight. They are wonderful people, but.... The Jews are just a very aggressive and abrasive and obnoxious personality.

The release of the Nixon tapes during the 1970s Watergate scandal marked the beginning of a sea of change in the way that people viewed the presidency. Up until then, the public had been used to seeing and hearing the president only in his finest moments—polished speeches and polished shoes, perfectly cut suits, and confident, well-rehearsed answers to carefully vetted questions.

But with Nixon, that idea of the presidency became a relic. Now, once a statement or photo gets into the information highway, there's no turning back, which means a presidential candidate's imprint has already been left bare for all to see.

One of the lowest points in the presidency occurred during the 1999 Monica Lewinsky scandal. It took place before the arrival of social media, but during an era of reporting that still made the story a part of everyone's daily lives. The old ways were still ingrained in President Bill Clinton's mindset: he had made a mistake and been caught, but he did his best to sweep it under the rug. In the new media age, his attempts to conceal and misdirect only exacerbated the situation. If Bill Clinton had stopped trying to appear "presidential" and simply admitted to the public that he'd had an extramarital affair with an intern, if he had been more authentic, more real, chances are he would be remembered differently today. The entire episode would be nothing but a footnote in the story of his life, instead of occupying the multiple chapters that it does today.

Interestingly, the night before the House of Representatives waged a debate to impeach President Clinton for lying to the grand jury, House Speaker-elect Bob Livingston, who was eager to boot Clinton out of office, told his colleagues that he had strayed from his marriage and had multiple affairs. Livingston felt he was left with little choice after Larry Flynt, who offered $1 million for evidence of sexual scandals among politicians, was on the brink of publishing an exposé of Livingston's affairs. He resigned from his position and was applauded for the way he handled his past transgressions. This allowed Livingston to maintain a higher level of respect from the public than if he had continued to pretend to have a flawless record. He stopped being congressional and started being *real*. Many felt that Clinton should have followed the same path because it would've saved both his wife and the country a lot of unnecessary aggravation, both then and even now.

Today, owning one's mistakes is de rigueur. With new media options seemingly proliferating by the day, President Obama has taken advantage of appearing on niche podcasts and intimate web comedy series. He is known to listen to rap, particularly Jay Z and Kendrick Lamar, which makes him seem more authentic. These days—chalk it up to reality TV—the public expects to see glimpses into the private lives of political figures. The flip side to this phenomenon is that younger generations no longer expect perfection from their leaders. This has a parallel in our celebrity culture, in which famous people appear in public, warts and all, never apologizing for their bad behavior, which often involves taking selfies in their bathroom mirrors. Mistakes that used to be glossed over are now claimed proudly. Public errors are part of life for public figures, and it seems that a person today would rather own the mistake than pretend it didn't actually happen.

NARCISSISM: MORE COMMON THAN YOU THINK

This is the social media climate that Donald Trump has willingly entered. By nature, he has no qualms about displaying his worst traits and owning them unapologetically. In fact, carrying himself in such a way has led many to call him a narcissist. According to *Psychology Today*, here are seven things only narcissists do:

- Assume everyone adores them.
- Make it clear they know everything.
- Insist on being the exception to the rule.
- Project an image of superiority.
- Make a great first impression, but quickly wear out their welcome.
- Boost their egos by implying others are inferior.
- Put their own feelings ahead of other people's needs.

How many apply to other presidential candidates, or athletes we adore, or celebrities we follow? Most of us carry at least one narcissistic trait, and Trump is no exception. However, to say that all seven of these describe the Republican frontrunner is over-the-top; and to imply they certainly apply to him in a greater extent than the presidential candidate who set up her own email server or the president who has a kill list is laughable.

One issue that many wonder about is his apparent lack of empathy. The public spotlight has shone for decades upon his business career and his place in the entertainment world, which is why we often miss the empathetic side of him that many doubt exists. Remember that he spent seven years remorselessly firing people on a television program, and this "reality television" show largely imprinted the image that we regard today as the real Donald Trump.

But it was also Donald Trump who took Jennifer Hudson under his wing when her mother, brother, and nephew were gunned down in Chicago, offering her a free apartment at Trump Tower while she grieved. She was never charged for her stay and was able to feel safe.

In 1988, Trump helped 3-year-old Andrew Ten, a boy who needed to fly to New York for special medical attention. The airline refused to let him board the plane because of his bulky medical equipment. Trump was informed of the issue and immediately sent his private jet to take the boy to New York.

In 1986, a woman named Annabell Hill was in danger of losing her family farm. Her husband had committed suicide in the misguided hope that his life insurance policy settlement would make their farm solvent. Trump heard about this woman's plight and offered enough financial help to make sure she could keep her farm, which had been in the Hill family for three generations.

PLANES, STEAK & WATER

After being arrested at the Mexican border with weapons in his car in 2013, Marine vet Andrew Tahmooressi spent seven months in a Mexican prison, where he was beaten and chained to a bed. When he was released, Trump sent him a check for $25,000 to help get him back on his feet.

Darnell Barton was driving his bus across a bridge when he spotted a woman preparing to jump. He stopped the bus, approached the woman, and convinced her not to take her own life that day. When Trump heard about the story, he sent Barton $10,000, commenting, "I thought that was so beautiful to see. I think he is a great guy with an amazing heart and I said that man should be rewarded."

Contrary to popular media belief, Donald Trump actually has a long history of helping others, as evidenced by Ivanka Trump in her RNC speech:

Over the years, on too many occasions to count, I saw my father tear stories out of the newspaper about people whom he had never met, who were facing some injustice or hardship. He'd write a note to his assistant, in a signature black felt tip pen, and request that the person be found and invited to Trump Tower to meet with him. He would talk to them and then draw upon his extensive network to find them a job or get them a break. And they would leave his office, as people so often do after having been with Donald Trump, feeling that life could be great again.

Because of Trump's innate generosity and empathy, he will likely listen to all Americans, not just his base (he has already begun to do so) and make intelligent decisions—though the bluntness and forcefulness of his speech may lead some to believe otherwise. Time and again, Trump has displayed his innate generosity. His expressions of empathy, particularly those expressed through financial gifts, seem unusually generous when compared to those of most national public office holders. And, lest you think it is because congressional members are not wealthy, remember that the Washington Post educated us on the matter in October of 2012,

Most members weathered the financial crisis better than the average American, who saw median household net worth drop 39 percent from 2007 to 2010. The median estimated wealth of members of the current Congress rose 5 percent during the same period, according to their reported assets and liabilities. The wealthiest one-third of Congress gained 14 percent.

Whether he is helping families in need or recognizing small acts of heroism or kindness, it's clear that Donald listened and lives in accordance with the idea that "to whom much is given, much will be required." In the same way, he will likely listen to Americans and make intelligent decisions—though the bluntness and forcefulness of his persona may lead some to believe otherwise.

It's also true that many of Trump's unique personality traits may make him seem "un-presidential," but he's the best person for the job in our rapidly changing world. In fact, there have been many candidates in the past who could have learned a thing or two from Trump's straightforward, unrehearsed approach. If they'd tried harder to be real people, as opposed to appearing "presidential," votes may have swung in their favor.

Consider Ted Cruz, who many felt would be an excellent Republican candidate. The Texas senator worked hard to carve out a niche as the most constitutionally centered conservative candidate on the stage. He was disciplined, setting up a campaign that mimicked Barack Obama's 2008 campaign apparatus. Senator Cruz also stuck with his anti-establishment message. Cruz's campaign believed its unmatched data operation and ground game, along with his popularity among grassroots conservatives, were enough to clinch the nomination. Like Bernie Sanders, most of his fundraising (intentionally) came from small, individual donations. Cruz connected with the grassroots, and his plan was to unite Tea Partiers and evangelicals under the same roof. In many ways, he succeeded when he won the Iowa primary. But this win turned out to be short-lived. As Barack Obama's chief strategist David Axelrod said,

"Cruz has run a clever, tactical race. He identified a discreet cohort—evangelicals and very conservative voters—and worked them relentlessly, which pays dividends in a huge and divided Iowa field. But the Trump wave overwhelmed tactics, the field dwindled, and Cruz found himself scrambling to enlarge his base."

Some analysts believe that Cruz was simply drowned out in the tidal wave of media coverage given to Donald Trump (Cruz echoed this belief himself in a podcast cast titled *OFF MESSAGE*). Many of his supporters and possibly Cruz himself believe that absent Trump—and his free media—he would have handily earned the Republican nomination; but that assessment, as usual, sold short Trump's intelligence and relentlessness.

Another person who fit the classic presidential profile was Dennis Hastert, the Republican politician from Illinois and the 51st Speaker of the United States House of Representatives. He represented Illinois in the House for 20 years, from 1987 to 2007. On paper, his record was sterling. He graduated from Wheaton College and went on to receive a master's degree in education from Northern Illinois University. For almost 15 years, Hastert was a high school teacher and coach, before he entered politics and won a seat in the Illinois House of Representatives in 1981. Six years later, he was elected to the United States House of Representatives. While there, he became chief deputy whip, which is the highest appointed position in the House. Eventually, he became Speaker of the House, which is the most powerful position in Congress and third in line to the presidency.

In fact, Hastert did sound like a president in the making—at least until the public found out the real truth about his private life. In May 2015, public accusations emerged that Hastert had sexually abused four male students when he was a teacher, and it was rumored that he was secretly paying one for his silence. After much prying, Hastert finally admitted that he had sexually abused teenage boys. The judge described him as a "serial child molester." Although he wasn't jailed for those particular crimes, he *was* fined and sentenced to 15 months in prison for his crime of structuring the withdrawal of $1 million in cash to avoid the bank's requirement of reporting transactions exceeding $10,000. Hastert is now known as one of the highest-ranking politicians in American history to be sentenced to prison.

Contrast that with the current Republican nominee. If there's one person who doesn't have a perfect record and never pretended to, it is Donald Trump. People may not agree with what he says or how he says it, but they don't have to question the *realness* of it. The Republican Party traditionally chooses a candidate who is the "perfect" conservative, someone with an impeccable record in government and, above all, who is a bona fide part of the establishment. In 2016, that mold finally broke. Registered Republicans and non-registered voters who leaned Republican had at last grown tired of the candidates who pasted on fake smiles and spoke like robots as they strived to appear "presidential" on the surface.

None of this is to say that all people in politics or the media have devastating skeletons in their closets. Instead, it's meant to encourage you, as voters, to embrace candidates that are a little rough around the edges. These are the candidates that you can trust; they aren't trying to shine themselves up to project an image. A candidate like Donald Trump embraces who he is and rarely apologizes for behavior; that may be considered, by some, as un-presidential. Donald Trump has no interest in pursuing

PLANES, STEAK & WATER

that particular adjective, though, because he seems unable to be disingenuous and because he knows that this would mean death to his brand.

Case in point: *The New York Times* conducted brief interviews of voters in August 2015. Jan Mannarino, a retired teacher from Michigan, said, "Even if he doesn't win, he's teaching other politicians to stop being politicians. He comes on strong. He could say it gently. But I think no one would listen." She seems to believe his defiance of political norms is his most admirable quality. Likewise, Carl Tomanelli, a retired NYC police officer who now lives in New Hampshire, said, "People are starting to see, I believe, that all this political correctness is garbage. I think he's echoing what a lot of people feel and say." Even his detractors admire these qualities. Paul Mittermeier, a Cincinnati voter, said, "I'm not personally a Trump supporter, but I think Trump's galvanizing rhetoric, his brute honesty, might be the selling point. He doesn't play the game that the rest of the establishment candidates do. He doesn't play the civility game."

There may even be scientific evidence that authentic people are better equipped to handle stressful jobs; this is related to a phenomenon known as *decision fatigue*. This compromising of our ability to think clearly sets in when there are too many decisions that have to be made in a given day, the kind of scenario that successful people often encounter. Perhaps those who aren't being true to themselves are worn down from the stress of pretending to be someone they are not. Imagine if you had to be false every minute of every workday, if you had to mentally poll-check every answer to every question. It would be exhausting. This is why some successful entrepreneurs wear the same clothing every day—Steve Jobs' famous black turtleneck, for instance. In effect, "automating" these decisions frees up the mind for less mundane tasks. By wearing a suit every day, even the president doesn't have to choose from anything more stressful than the color of a necktie. Donald Trump won't have such decision fatigue because he is totally, unapologetically himself in every situation, and this may account for some of his boundless energy; he only sleeps about four hours per night.

Perhaps Trump's lack of political experience also somewhat accounts for his uncensored, honest persona on the campaign trail. But this is not a liability to his supporters. Rather, this is one of the main reasons they want to send him to Washington. A significant number of Americans are feeling real pain and need someone to address the issues affecting their lives. For example, while unemployment is technically at just over 5 percent of the population, almost 60 percent of America's workforce is paid hourly and works only part-time. The majority of part-time employees are doing low-wage work at jobs that typically provide less than a week's notice for scheduling. These people are not counted in the ranks of the unemployed.

These numbers may not affect you, but they certainly wreak havoc on the single mother who needs to provide childcare while she works behind the register. Or the man who works in the stockyard and needs to make sure he can afford an algebra tutor so his son can move on to the next grade. Or the woman who needs regular dialysis treatments but also needs to keep her job at the local diner.

To fix these problems, America doesn't need a president who makes promises that he or she can't keep. Instead, America needs jobs—more of them, higher-paying ones, full-time ones. To accomplish this, we need a president with *experience creating jobs*, rather than experience lecturing students (think Obama) or someone whose only or primary career has been in politics (think Hillary and Sanders). We need someone who can take the problems real people are facing, make difficult decisions, and embrace the kind of changes that create economic opportunity.

In this sense, Donald Trump is a brash breath of fresh air. People are eager for such a shift in our presidential candidates, particularly after decades of empty promises that have resulted in little benefit to those struggling to stay in the middle class. They crave a leader who may be rough around the edges, but whose statements don't need parsing. And while he makes many flubs—most of his errors are unforced—he could certainly learn to own those errors in an authentic way, which will continue to endear people to him.

In one sense, Trump has inoculated himself against the outrage that the left has regularly heaped upon the Republican candidates' stated policies. While Republican campaigns have had just as much mudslinging as Democratic campaigns, Republican *candidates* have traditionally been squeaky clean. This has made them sitting ducks for charges of hypocrisy. Remember the clean-cut Mitt Romney, the very picture of a cautious executive, whose statements never offended anybody? He was caught on videotape at a private fundraiser noting that 47 percent of the American public was essentially dead weight, contributing nothing. This gave Democrats an opportunity to pounce, and they took it. Truth is never a defense for being unauthentic. Trump, however, has deployed a brilliant strategy—whether by accident or intentionally—by making such openly outrageous statements to begin with; he has usurped the ability of the Democrats to win with notions that a candidate may or may not be sincere.

The sanitized candidate is dead. The votes of the future belong to the authentic.

If the world should blow itself up, the last audible voice would be that of an expert saying it can't be done.

—PETER USTINOV

CHAPTER 5

PLEASE DON'T FEEL SO STUPID

SITTING IN HIS wheelchair next to the hospital window, Jim Sack reflected on the day that he had left East High School in Denver to enlist in the Navy. There was something about the way the blue sky met the lush green grass that reminded him of that afternoon 50 years ago, a time when he was a young man ready to tackle the world.

Sack was initially stationed in California and later aboard an aircraft carrier that cruised to the Gulf of Tonkin, where he served as an air crewman. Sack loved the high seas, the breathtaking expanse, the exciting storms, and the unique scent of salt air when far from land.

At 67 years old, Sack learned that he needed major spinal cord surgery and expected to be admitted to the new VA hospital near Denver, Colorado—not far from home. Unfortunately, that hospital was still under construction, so Sack had to travel to Long Beach, California for surgery in March of 2015.

On his way to the airport, Sack drove past the construction site of the new Denver VA hospital and was pleased to see the construction workers. "I think it's a very good thing. This will be updated, all fresh and all. It's going to be a lot better than Ninth and Claremont," he said.

Another Colorado veteran, James Weaver, recalled the day he had decided to enlist. The infamous Pearl Harbor attack on December 7, 1941, inspired him to reconsider the path he was taking in life. He had come from a family of fishermen and "always liked the water." After a little pushing from his adopted father, a World War I sailor, Weaver signed on for a tour with the Navy.

Almost two years later, on September 4, 1943, Weaver was on a ship near New Guinea when it was hit by a torpedo. The explosion forced his ship upward, killed six men aboard, and broke Weaver's back. He spent five months in the hospital before returning to service and then stayed in the Navy for the next 12 and a half years. Now, Weaver hopes to live long enough to see the new hospital built in Denver. "It should have been built years ago," he said. "These bigwigs say, 'I'm going to do this,' and then tomorrow, they say something else. The VA should not be in the hospital business."

Sack and Weaver are two examples of both young and older veterans who would benefit from the finished VA hospital outside of Denver. A plan was put in motion over 10 years ago to replace the old, crowded facilities for nearly 400,000 vets in Colorado and neighboring states. The VA initially budgeted $328 million for the state-of-the-art facility, but that quickly proved to be an unrealistic number. Over a decade later, the project still isn't finished, with the price hitting $1.7 billion. It's currently one of the most expensive hospitals in the world. (Approximately 24,000 veterans living in Colorado are either homeless or unemployed; $1.7 billion would have solved those problems and more overnight. Instead, the money went to private corporations and, no doubt, bloated bureaucrat salaries.)

The VA is in the business of providing health care to veterans in all 50 states. They have been in charge of the construction of all necessary facilities, such as hospitals, and are trusted to do their job correctly. However, it turns out that the VA has been falling behind on this construction job, along with many others. The cost overruns have been enormous, for which the VA has cited multiple factors ranging from low initial estimates to poor planning to repeated delays. They recently handed the project over to the Army Corps of Engineers (after the initial contractor walked away due to breach of contract issues). The Engineering Corps is expected to complete the hospital by 2018. However, maybe it's time to take things into our own hands.

By electing a president with a proven track record in construction—someone who knows how to deal with budgets, contractors, and countless big government regulations—we can reduce the chance of these shameful fiascos occurring. Enter Donald Trump. It's not merely Trump's expertise as a construction manager that we need in a president. It is his practical, real-world experience that gives him a knack for and commitment to *getting things done*. As opposed to the world of law books and theory that spawned Barack Obama, or congressional interns and speechwriters that spawned Paul Ryan and so many other professional politicians, and which may well account for their inability to launch a website, stabilize health care, deal with criminal justice reform or pass meaningful tax reform—in short, *get things done*. They have never "done" much of anything except think and talk about what they're thinking. The left seems to believe that we need an Intellectual-In-Chief in the White House, but, unfortunately the size and scope of government (which both party establishments are responsible for growing) calls for a Project-Manager-In-Chief.

The media seldom misses the chance to parade before us a myriad of "experts." Though we want to believe that the people who stand in front of cameras and are quoted in newspapers have solutions to pressing issues, these are the people that often fail our country.

These so-called experts often lack concrete success in their fields—most of those with concrete success go into the private sector. While some people can spend a lifetime researching the theories behind solutions—and we should admire that—it doesn't really amount to boots-on-the-ground, practical knowledge. Would you rather trust your car to a mechanic who has a successful track record of inspecting, diagnosing, and repairing automobiles or a guy who has read *Car & Driver* magazine for a few years and "has a theory"?

Academics and other experts can offer theoretical perspectives that may help our leaders make sound decisions. However, the folks on the ground who have spent years hip-deep in getting things done are often more useful. In other words, the people who have created jobs, opened businesses, hired and fired employees, signed a general liability policy, and fought the IRS for what is rightfully theirs have the sort of *practical* knowledge so lacking in many of our political leaders. For instance, Bernie Sanders nearly became the Democratic presidential nominee. However, outside of his political experience, what has he accomplished without the backing of a government paycheck? Also, take a look at Barack Obama's career pre-presidency. He taught school, was an activist, and spent three years as a U.S. senator (not even completing a full term). How do these things make him any more qualified than Donald Trump? And, last but not least, what about Hillary Clinton? Sure, she has spent countless hours in meetings, networking and hobnobbing; she has made all the connections one needs with world leaders. And she, no doubt, knows every acronym that comes with a lifetime of living off the government dole. However, has any of her expertise or that of her chief supporter, President Obama, actually connected them with Americans on the ground? When there was a government shutdown, their lights were still on, and they still had food in their belly. Let your company shut down, even briefly; how long before you can't make a light bill payment? Do these career politicians understand that, at best, upward mobility for most of us in this country has flatlined—that where we are born is probably where we will die? Secretary Clinton and President Obama have guaranteed six-figure paychecks for life; and, they have never come close, in their careers, to truly being broke, busted, and disgusted. Unlike Trump, they risk your money every day but will live like kings, results be damned. It is particularly funny how everyone is an expert with somebody else's money.

Look at the federal government, in particular. This behemoth has grown exponentially over the last century. In 2015, all government spending, including federal, state, and local, accounted for over 34 percent of gross domestic product (GDP) spending. Since the GDP represents the total dollar value of all goods and services produced, it can be argued that the government accounts for *a third of our total spending in the United States!*

The government is, indeed, a formidable beast, and the political system that feeds into it is immensely complicated. A politician or academic who claims to have fully grasped every facet of politics is either foolish or dishonest. To be an "expert" on gun control, environmental issues, education, foreign affairs, and agriculture is nothing short of impossible. Part of the problem is that the very meaning of the word *expertise* has become watered-down, particularly with the rise of search engines. More and more, American culture has shifted into a "Google-fueled, Wikipedia-based, blog-sodden collapse of any division between professionals and laymen, students and teachers, knowers and wonderers—in other words, between those of any achievement in an area and those with none at all," as Tom Nichols noted in an article in *The Federalist* entitled "The Death of Expertise."

To make matters worse, people often spend more time trying to make others feel stupid than they do proving a point. Politicians often trot out polysyllabic, convoluted terminology in an apparent effort to fool the American public into buying whatever political snake oil they are selling. *He must know what he's talking about*, we think. It is so arcane and complicated that we are impressed and swayed. George Orwell wrote about this in his timeless essay *Politics and the English Language*, in which he said that politicians, journalists, and academics use meaningless words to make lies sound truthful. Connor Lynch wrote an article for AlterNet, in which he argues that politicians throw around six terms—*socialism, centrism, patriotism, terrorism, collateral damage*, and *job creators*—so often and so loosely that they've lost their meaning and should be banned from the political arena.

REAL TALK VS. TALKING POINTS

Even sadder is the fact that often politicians don't even realize that such words are mere campaign talking points. For example, political experts lamented Trump's refusal to mount a traditional primary campaign, as he failed to script himself or his surrogates and, by doing so, gave himself considerable leeway to answer questions, engage with media, and be forthright (rather than scripted). In other words, we got to see a real human responding in real time—not always pretty, accurate, or stated in the most profound way, but certainly *real*. Trump, no doubt, wanted to avoid Joe Scarborough's lament, "the echo of a thousand focus groups," that you could hear in Marco Rubio's campaign. Every American should praise him for this effort.

Trump may not be an expert in government, but in the field of real estate ventures, he has surpassed 10,000 hours of study and application, which is the benchmark set in the book *Peak* by Anders Ericsson (made famous by Malcolm Gladwell in *Outliers*). In fact, Trump has tried his hand at a large number of business ventures, which we'll look at in a later chapter. Of course, not all were successful, but most of his greatest successes have relied upon his greatest strength: real estate.

What does it take to be a successful real estate developer? In the *Houston Chronicle*, Ronald Kimmons advises the path one must take. Step 1 is attaining a degree in a field such as finance. To this end, Trump graduated from the University of Pennsylvania's famed Wharton School of Finance in 1968. Step 2 is getting hired by an employer already in the real estate business. For several years, Trump labored under his father, who owned various apartment buildings in the New York City area. Once he had a grip on the world of building demolition, steel framing, structural systems, and RevPAR, he wanted to take business to the next level. That is when he established his own brand, which is Step 3.

Trump has taken a practical, demanding path, forging an incredible career in the process. It's undeniable that he is a successful "doing" expert in the field of real estate. That being said, an essential question presents itself: How does this translate into presidential qualification?

Here's how. Steps 4 through 6 suggest that a successful real estate developer work with construction firms or professional contractors. Kimmons particularly recommends building relationships with local and independent lenders to finance investment activities at the best rate possible.

Trump has displayed a knack for building positive relationships with others—be they New York City bureaucrats, construction workers, bank financers, or tenants—in order to complete massive, complicated projects. Though he oversees innumerable operations and encounters daunting challenges along the way, he negotiates as necessary and nearly always completes the task at hand, unless faced with superhuman obstacles. Because of this, there is no doubt that he makes many difficult and time-sensitive decisions along the way, which is why it is vital that he rely upon the most qualified people to supply him with the data needed to make those decisions.

Perhaps the real truth is that voters don't want to know their politicians' plans in any detail. Voters just want to know that politicians have plans, that they believe in them passionately, and that they intend to accomplish something.

The alternative would be for Trump to spout a bunch of policy wonk details that would bore and baffle his supporters (and the American public, in general). However, that's not how elections are won, and that isn't his style. Personality trumps, so to speak, intellectual obfuscation.

This works to Trump's advantage. He knew going into this race that he was less knowledgeable on foreign policy than Hillary Clinton, who served as Secretary of State for four years. In fact, he stated again and again that he had no immediate plans to run for president. "But then something changed," Jonah Goldberg wrote in the *National Review*. "One too many followers said, 'Do it!' One too many valets whispered, 'America needs you'—probably just before asking for a raise." Whatever it was, Trump decided that he didn't necessarily need to have all the answers to stand a fighting chance. He had mastered new challenges before this, and he knew that he could master another.

The experience argument doesn't hold much water since, in actuality, only a few of our presidents have had foreign policy experience, and many didn't even have business experience. President Obama had no experience turning a profit. Although he had sat on some notable boards and was founder and president of an educational nonprofit, he had zero business or foreign policy experience. George W. Bush and Bill Clinton also had no foreign policy experience, so they did the same as every president before them (and the same as Donald Trump will do)—that is, seek counsel from those who they believe can offer the best advice.

What complicates matters further is the fact that many government career bureaucrats, whom all White House residents rely upon to execute orders, tend to lean ideologically left. This is not a pejorative statement, as studies show that the majority of government employee donations are given to Democratic Party candidates. Thus, these donations continue with each president, regardless of the president's political affiliation; and these bureaucrats execute ground-level enforcement that affects American families. This is because career bureaucrats, as liberals, believe that the government is the best answer to all problems; whereas, Republicans believe in shaving down government jobs, and high-achieving conservatives tend to prefer private industry to government service.

Take a minute and consider the elected presidents of the last century. Many of them succeeded in passing successful legislation or leading the nation through crises, but many of those same presidents also ushered in ideas, programs, and laws that were crushingly stupid. For example, Woodrow Wilson signed the Volstead Act, the enforcement arm of the 18th Amendment that prohibited the manufacture, transportation, and sale of alcohol. John F. Kennedy failed to authorize air support for the invasion of the Bay of Pigs, resulting in the loss of hundreds of American troops and a victory for Fidel Castro. Jimmy Carter failed to negotiate the release of 52 American citizens in Iran. In the Watergate scandal, Richard Nixon was caught authorizing people to pose as plumbers to break into Democratic Party headquarters. After Osama bin Laden attacked the United States on September 11, George W. Bush led the charge to invade Iraq, which was unconnected to the terrorist act, though some of his intelligence personnel tried to persuade him otherwise. All were considered experts who knew the political system—how to manage their own bureaucracies and dance politely with foreign powers.

Is it possible that *nobody* was giving well-balanced intelligence to these deciders? Were they all locked in echo chambers of groupthink? Joe Scarborough certainly seems to think so. In 2013, he went on a rant on MSNBC, sarcastically attacking President Obama for continuing the Bush/Cheney legacy. "Thank God he got elected," Scarborough said. "You know the world loves us so much more today than they did." Then he abruptly dropped the sarcasm. "You people are all jokes! This is what you got—you got a drone dropping, phone-tapping president!"

Many of the media elite, such as Scarborough, forget that the so-called "experts" have led our country down many unpredictable and destructive paths.

Trump, meanwhile, has a radically different outlook. He's a bull in a china shop, true, but what's overlooked is that this bull has the ability to bring about the kind of change that career politicians simply can't accomplish.

For instance, he brags that he's not an expert in the political field. He doesn't attempt to hide it, and he doesn't obfuscate in order to trick the American public into thinking he's something that he's not. He said to a Charlotte, North Carolina crowd of supporters, "As you know, I am not a politician ... I've never wanted to learn the language of the insiders, and I've never been politically correct—it takes far too much time..." Indeed, political frontrunners no longer aim to demonstrate their expertise;

they simply want to sound good. According to political fact checker Angie Drobnic Holan, all politicians lie, just some more than others. Holan puts statements into one of five categories: True/Mostly True, Half False/Half True, Mostly False, False, and Pants on Fire. In a chart that tracks statements made by presidential candidates since 2007, it's easy to see how loose most politicians are with their facts.

President Obama may be the most fact-checked person by PolitiFact, with 569 of his statements checked. Nine of those fall into the Pants on Fire category, which refers to the most outrageous falsehoods. For example, President Obama said, "We've got close to 7 million Americans who have access to health care for the first time because of Medicaid expansion," while, in reality, perhaps half that many people are enjoying such benefits. Hillary Clinton also claimed, "I'm the only candidate in the Democratic primary, or actually on either side, who Wall Street financiers and hedge fund managers are actually running ads against." However, that whopper is not likely to fool many voters, even Democrats.

Donald Trump is not above making exaggerated statements. He once commented on unemployment, saying, "Don't believe those phony numbers when you hear 4.9 and 5 percent unemployment. The number's probably 28, 29, as high as 35. In fact, I even heard recently 42 percent." Although there is no doubt Trump heard that statement, the real number (according to most job analysts) is closer to 11 percent. Most of us realized that without independent verification.

Falsehoods are falsehoods, and exaggerated claims are exaggerated claims. However, the significant difference between the broad statements of Trump and Clinton is that Trump has never claimed to be an expert, and he acknowledges that he is learning as he goes. Also, after so many failures by established "expert" politicians, why would he want to be lumped in with them? One of his greatest strengths is his outsider perspective—one that doesn't carry any of the typical biases or agendas of a typical major party nominee.

A TRAIL OF UNBROKEN PROMISES

George H.W. Bush made an infamous promise on the campaign trail in 1988 when he said, "Read my lips: no new taxes." This, when combined with his status as Reagan's vice president, sealed the deal for him to win the election. However, he was hung out to dry by his own words four years later when he signed a tax increase.

A young upstart and former governor of Arkansas named Bill Clinton vociferously attacked this lie during the 1992 presidential campaign, which helped earn him the presidency. Ironically, Clinton ran into the same problem when he promised healthcare reform during his presidency, delivering a major speech to Congress in September of 1993 that detailed universal health care. He chose Hillary Clinton to lead the task force and sell the plan to the public, but the plan backfired, and the program never came to fruition. The Democrats suffered terrible losses in the midterm elections that year.

So much for the effectiveness of a married expert *team*.

A lot is said during a presidential campaign, but history shows the unlikelihood of those words leading to action. Keep in mind that unmet campaign promises, in and of themselves, don't indicate the failure or success of a president. After all, George H.W. Bush had a 90 percent approval rating when he made the tough decision in 1990 to cobble together an allied force that would toss Saddam Hussein out of Kuwait.

When we look at Trump's résumé, we see a man who has

characteristics that are attractive in a president. One could ask, though, "Can he successfully change careers?" Let's examine some high-profile, high-power people who've made such a change and see how they fared.

Consider Bill Gates, who stepped away from Microsoft, the tech company he helped found and build to world prominence, to start the Bill & Melinda Gates Foundation. As the world's richest man, he certainly didn't need to make a change, but his desire to bring about change and contribute to the welfare of others became his mission. Today, his philanthropic organization is one of the most successful in history.

Consider also Martha Stewart. Long before she was a media darling, she worked as a model for Chanel and later took a position on Wall Street selling securities at the brokerage firm Monness, Horstman, Williams, and Sidel. Then, she took an interest in renovating her family's Connecticut home, which was her gateway to the catering and entertaining business. Opportunities arose, and she ran with them.

Jeff Bezos is another example of a successful career change. After college, he worked on Wall Street in the computer science field and then built a network for an international trade company. To make his mark on Internet commerce, he wrote the business plan for Amazon, set up the company in his garage, left his high-paying New York City job, and went on to change the world of online retailing.

However, sometimes, even those who are still active in their field end up losing ground and expertise. Technology moves quickly in today's globalized world, and with it moves the knowledge of human experience. One of the most obvious ways we can see this radical change is in medicine. Although countless examples exist to illustrate a former expert falling behind on the job, this can be easily shown through medical comedy.

The NBC/ABC show *Scrubs* involves hilarity saturated with real-life emotions. Episode 14 of Season 2 involved Dr. Townshend, played by the incomparable Dick Van Dyke. Townshend is the star, class clown, jokester, and good ol' boy of the hospital. He's been around forever. Everybody—and we do mean everybody—loves this guy.

In a surprising turn of events, Townshend accepts a patient and suggests surgery, unaware that the patient can be easily treated by a modern, less-invasive medical procedure. Zach Braff, playing the lovable and awkward young Dr. John Dorian, is shocked when the older gentleman suggests using an old-school procedure. Townshend instructs Dorian in the procedure, which goes horribly wrong. The older doctor says that he'll "take the blame" for practically butchering a patient's neck.

Dear Dr. Dorian can't handle the guilt that plagues him after this near-disaster. He, a capable yet powerless medical intern, caused serious damage to a real patient! But wasn't he supposed to follow instructions? Wasn't Townshend, the most senior member of the hospital staff (and highly favored, at that), to be trusted? Wasn't he the *expert*?

At the last minute, our hero decides to come clean and tell his supervisor, Dr. Kelso, about his mistake—and about the misguided instructions from the celebrated Dr. Townsend that led him to it. We cringe as he does this right in front of Dr. Townshend, and the whole situation ends up as an embarrassing joke at Dorian's expense.

Later in the episode, the hospital supervisor looks into Dr. Townshend's records and discovers that Townsend's treatments are out-of-date, dangerous even. When Dr. Townshend shamefully admits that he has no intention of keeping up with medical advances, the supervisor removes him from the doctors' rotation with a heavy heart.

In this episode, *Scrubs* teaches us that even a renowned expert can be the least qualified man for the job. It's not about age, and it's certainly not about being "in the thick of it." A one-time expert can easily fall behind the times right from the operating table. Experts need continuing education just like the rest of us. We can't trust their expertise at face value.

The common thread of all of this is that successful people are successful people. They are able to transition from one field to the next, not without struggle or having to learn new methods or procedures, but with the confidence that they'll be on top once again. Many people are experts before ever even entering their careers. However, with the tools, ambition, and wherewithal to be successful, this expertise doesn't matter. Donald Trump isn't an expert on government, but he has what's necessary to make the transition. He is a brilliant, hard-working world-changer, a doer, a *Git Er Done,* and yes, a winner.

In a large way, Trump is running the most honest campaign in history, which is something the elite media should be praising him for. He is limited in his political knowledge (and knows it), but he isn't afraid of his limitations. Instead, Trump plans to do what he has always done as a wildly successful businessman— that is, surround himself with the best and brightest to get the job done right while always being open to adapting and changing while marching for success. Instead of fighting his lack of expertise, Trump will, and must, embrace it.

Interfering in someone else's argument
is as foolish as yanking a dog's ears.

—Proverbs 26:17

CHAPTER 6

BUTTINSKY

WHILE DONALD TRUMP has done an awful lot of talking off the cuff, he has remained consistent in his broader ideas concerning foreign policy. To fully understand his way of thinking, which runs counter to our current dogma, we need to go back 80 years—almost four generations—to the presidency of Franklin Delano Roosevelt.

Years before the Japanese attacked the United States at Pearl Harbor, drawing our nation into World War II, the nations that would later form the Axis powers had already begun their wars of aggression. In 1935, Mussolini sent his Italian forces to conquer Ethiopia. In 1936, Nazi troops invaded the Rhineland, and Germany annexed Austria two years later. In 1937, Japan committed the horrific Rape of Nanking. At the 1938 Munich Conference, Britain and France surrendered Czechoslovakia's Sudetenland. Roosevelt condemned international acts of aggression after he took office in 1933, but he did little more. The American public remained haunted by the trench-war carnage of the "Great War," and Roosevelt sensed that they had no interest in being involved in another such conflagration.

Roosevelt was, in fact, correct. The majority of the American people were exhausted and, thus, antiwar. In 1934, Congress passed the Johnson Act, which prohibited loans to nations that had fallen behind on World War I debt repayment (a move that ultimately helped bring to power Adolf Hitler). The Neutrality

Act, passed in 1935, blocked the export of arms, ammunition, or implements of war to belligerent nations. A 1937 amendment forbade American citizens and ships from entering war zones or traveling on belligerents' ships. The United States was doing all it could to stay out of the world's problems.

When Hitler invaded Poland in violation of previous agreements, and Europe erupted in a firefight that quickly became World War II, Roosevelt knew Germany had to be stopped. He also knew that Americans did not have the will to do it. He promised that the United States would not fight unless attacked, but nonetheless braced the country for what might come by increasing the defense budget and effectively converting America to a military economy. Roosevelt also stacked his cabinet with interventionists such as Henry Stimson (Secretary of War) and Frank Knox (Secretary of Navy). Secret talks with Winston Churchill began, but it wasn't until bombs rained down that fateful morning in Hawaii that Congress and the nation realized they had no choice but to declare war.

Since then, it seems, our nation has pursued a policy in which everyone's business is our business. Our officially stated goals, as outlined in the Foreign Policy Agenda of the State Department, are "to build and sustain a more democratic, secure, and prosperous world for the benefit of the American people and the international community." The U.S. House Committee on Foreign Affairs stated that some of its jurisdictional goals were to:

…export controls, including nonproliferation of nuclear technology and nuclear hardware; measure to foster commercial interaction with foreign nations and to safeguard American business abroad; international commodity agreements; international education; and protection of American citizens abroad and expatriation.

Given that the United States found itself unwittingly thrust into a universal leadership position, it's understandable how the nation ended up on its current foreign policy path. Donald Trump, however, believes that we've been the world's policeman for too long. He senses that America has been getting a raw deal from the liberal international order it has led since 1945. Trump has voiced two key foreign policy points:

1. He is unhappy with military alliances and feels the United States is overcommitted around the world.

2. He believes America is disadvantaged in the new global economy.

These views are not new. In fact, Trump's first mention of such a policy was made public in 1987, when he paid $100,000 to run a *New York Times* ad detailing the ways he believed countries, such as Japan and Saudi Arabia, were taking advantage of the United States. "The world is laughing at America's politicians as we protect ships we don't own, carrying oil we don't need, destined for allies who won't help," he wrote. Ideas like this have been dormant in American politics for so long that people mistakenly believe they're as unique as Trump himself.

Trump is angry, and not necessarily only at our enemies. In a 1990 interview with *Playboy* magazine, he was asked what "President Trump's" foreign policy would look like. Trump responded,

He would believe very strongly in extreme military strength. He wouldn't trust anyone. He wouldn't trust the Russians; he wouldn't trust our allies; he'd have a huge military arsenal, perfect it, understand it. Part of the problem is that we're defending some of the wealthiest countries in the world for nothing. We're being laughed at around the world, defending Japan.

He repeated the point more forcefully:

We Americans are laughed at around the world for losing a hundred and fifty billion dollars year after year for defending wealthy nations for nothing, nations that would be wiped off the face of the earth in about fifteen minutes if it weren't for us. Our 'allies' are making billions screwing us.

In 2013, Trump criticized the United States' relationship with South Korea by saying, "How long will we go on defending South Korea from North Korea without payment? When will they start to pay us?" In an interview with NBC while on the campaign trail, Trump noted, "We have 28,000 soldiers on the line in South Korea between the madman and them. We get practically nothing compared to the cost of this."

Trump, in effect, is asking, is it wrong for America to get paid for its massive responsibility and contributions to the defense of the West? Are we burning money simply because we don't have the nerve and vision to change with the times? Did we get our money's worth in Libya, for instance, where "regime change" has led to death, turmoil, and instability? Remember the deaths of Ambassador Stevens, Sean Smith, Tyron Woods, and Glen Doherty? We can ask the same about many of the world's hotspots. The answer is unsettling.

In his worldview, Europe shouldn't be getting off scot-free either. The 28-member military alliance known as NATO (North Atlantic Treaty Organization), founded out of the devastation of World War II in the name of defense against the Soviet Union, is largely dependent on the United States. As the *Telegraph* (UK) wrote in a July 2016 article, "America's permanent commitment to protect Europe, embodied by the NATO alliance, amounts to the cornerstone of the continent's security."

Trump has been lambasted for his comments on NATO. Donald Trump said, "Pulling back from Europe would save this country millions of dollars annually. The cost of stationing

NATO troops in Europe is enormous." Trump's mere acknowl-edgement that we should question where, how, and for what purpose the American tax dollar is spent has the old order run-ning in a panic.

The United States contributes nearly one-fifth of NATO's budget. Why? Status? Does anyone believe that this equates to more status for us as a nation? Judging by our loyal European allies' frequent criticism, the answer is a resounding *no*. In March of 2015, Trump complained that Germany was not car-rying more of the financial burden of NATO and questioned the wisdom of the United States allowing Europe to lean on America so strongly for its security.

The United States deploys troops in over 150 nations around the world. Many countries—Canada, for instance—seem to see no need for a hearty defense budget as long as they know the United States will fight their battles for them. If the local neigh-borhood council gave you a free breakfast every morning, it would be foolish for you even to budget for your breakfast, and, after decades, your family might not think they need to pay for their own breakfast. Why is it so illogical to question the status quo?

Some argue that keeping troops stationed overseas is a less expensive proposition than having to deploy to hotspots on a moment's notice. True or not, these distinctions are neither here nor there in Trump's mind because he doesn't think the U.S. military should be the globe's social services department— at least not without payment. In his mind, the United States should have the best military in the world but abdicate its more recent role of ensuring open access to what are called the global commons: oceans, air, and space. For example, the U.S. Navy guarantees the openness of sea lanes for civilian trade. Trump believes that we should either stop acting as the police officers or, at the very least, receive payment for the duty.

Interestingly, though they are the "party of change," the Democrats seem to want to limit that change to internal policies. Their current candidate seems perfectly content that most aspects of U.S. foreign policy are rooted in Eisenhower-era thinking. But with the kind of reductions in foreign spending that Trump's policies would bring, how many VA hospitals could be built? How many highways updated, how many inner cities revitalized? As Trump said, "These are clearly funds that can be put to better use."

The point is this: The United States is providing a service to other countries in the realm of safety and protection. Americans wouldn't expect such a service for free, so why are we giving it away? For years, Trump's been ridiculing this. It's time we listened.

TRUMP AND RUSSIA

It's worth discussing Trump's attitude toward Russia as well. His belief is that we should keep ourselves close to Russia as an opportunity to fight terrorism but not necessarily capitulate on every issue. While many current experts (there are those experts again) consider Trump's strategy dangerous, most of them apparently forget that not only has the United States never been at war with Russia but that the Cold War is over. We should all remember the adage, "The enemy of my enemy is my friend." Consider World War II and our partnership with the "Soviet Devil" that beat back Nazi Germany. Without the USSR, the Allied powers more likely would have suffered far greater casualties (the USSR alone suffered 20 million casualties) and may have lost the war.

In this situation, Trump is reminding all of us to look at this differently. Despite the annexation of Crimea and despite our differences (which are far less profound than our disagreements with many so-called friendly nations), the United States can't afford to alienate Russia. And, perhaps, there is an even larger game afoot for Trump. It's possible, based upon his intelligence briefings, that he knows information that the public doesn't.

He has always been much savvier than most would give him credit for, and the many ways our interests align with Russia's have not escaped him. Petroleum and natural gas still power the global economy and probably will for quite some time to come. Russia is a major producer of both, and the European Union relies upon it for one-third of its oil needs. It is hard to pin down the thought processes behind any Trump foreign policy, but since the United States lifted limits on oil exports in 2015, perhaps Trump's long-term objective is to develop a working relationship with Russia, especially in the fossil fuels arena. For example, if Russia withheld exports from Europe, it would increase demand for U.S. oil exports and potentially drive up oil prices here in the United States, which would hurt our national psyche and national pocketbook since we've become comfortable with low oil prices and subsequent economic growth. Simply put, our economic boom, as paltry as it is, can be contributed in part to low oil prices here, and a friendship with Putin may be Trump's way of continuing that in the future.

Our myopic approach to Russia is one shared by both major parties. Remember how Mitt Romney called Russia "our number one geopolitical foe"? (Obama pushed back on that during one debate, but now our once would-be foe needs to become an ally, which is something Obama has yet to realize.) Hillary Clinton and the Democratic Party faithful have gone out of their way to demonize Putin, some even calling him a brutal dictator (when, in fact, at least according to Putin controlled media, he is an elected official who enjoys great popular support at home), conveniently forgetting how many actual dictators enjoy current favor from the Obama administration.

The other concern about standing with Russia is the number of atrocities that its allies have committed. The most notorious is Syria, of course, but Equatorial Guinea and Uganda are just two of the others. In particular, Uganda recently passed horrible anti-homosexuality laws and has witnessed a spate of brutal attacks, yet the United States has an embassy there, and we maintain diplomatic relations. Again, we remain friendly with many nations whose civil rights records are questionable. Why the double standard? Every American knows that Al Qaeda is our enemy, though we have recently provided weapons to an Al Qaeda-led rebellion against the Assad dictatorship in Syria, and, according to Russian Foreign Minister Lavrov, the United States asked Russia "not to hit" Al-Qaeda's Syrian branch!

So why the snarling at Trump about his reasonable approach to Russia? President Obama was able to change our official relationship with Cuba; the same should be possible with our attitude toward Russia. We should reject the fantasy of a return to the Cold War—beating back the hammer and sickle may have represented our nation's finest ideological hours, but that was then. We've changed, but we haven't grown.

A change to foreign policy as radical as Donald Trump's ideas gives one pause. This is understandable, but many foreign policy experts are frightened by any thinking that is outside their box, and their inability to embrace new paths in foreign policy has not served us well.

Remember this: foreign countries let us lead not because we are so great but because leadership in foreign policy requires great financial expenditures and sacrifice of lives, and they are more than willing to let us carry these burdens. Consider the war in Afghanistan. The raw cost of that war seems to be around

$1 trillion; however, once you include the long-term costs (such as interest on the debt), it probably will be closer to double that. Some have concluded (although there seems to be no exact figure) that there have been a total of 12,000 killed, both military and civilian, and more than 17,500 wounded. Many experts, such as Dean Stavridis of Tufts University, argue that Syria will have to be broken apart via Western intervention. No proponent of this view seems to understand that such an event represents a continuation of our failed policies. With the words of Albert Einstein not too far from our hearts, "Insanity is doing the same thing over and over again and expecting different results." Is there any wonder that Trump wants us to stop being the world's buttinsky?

My feelings about this are constantly evolving, I struggle with this.

—PRESIDENT BARACK H. OBAMA

CHAPTER 7

THE TRUTH ABOUT THE FLIP-FLOP

HAL HERZOG IS considered the world's number one anthrozoologist. He has spent the last 20 years studying interactions between humans and animals. Over that time, he's studied animal activists, cockfighters, animal researchers, circus animal trainers, and vegetarians.

The last category yielded some interesting results, particularly when Herzog studied vegetarians who returned to omnivorous lifestyles. Of all Herzog's subjects, none seemed to shock or surprise him as much as his daughter. After 18 years of committed vegetarianism, she asked her father for suggestions about which types of meat she might enjoy. He was fascinated, having seen her so often repulsed by steak, hamburgers, and chicken.

Herzog asked his daughter to jot down a few words about why she was compelled to change her ways. She explained that at 13, she had become a vegetarian as a way to feel different from other people in her small Southern town. However, after almost two decades of constantly feeling hungry, she had reached the point at which eating felt like a chore, much like doing the dishes or cleaning the bathroom. Other people around her seemed to have a deep love of food that she'd never experienced, and she wanted to know that feeling for herself.

Herzog's daughter is more the rule than the exception. In fact, five out of six vegetarians eventually abandon their meatless diets, with vegans slightly less likely to backslide: seven out of 10 eventually return to meat. Herzog advises those considering vegetarianism to cut back on their meat intake rather than eliminate it altogether. A vegetarian lifestyle is challenging for many reasons, and for those without the vigilance to ingest adequate quantities of vegetable protein, the lifestyle also represents a potential health hazard. Thus, many seemingly devoted vegetarians soon abandon the practice when practicality intersects ideology. They are humans—thinking, considering, ever evolving.

The fact is *people change*. Sometimes, people change rapidly and seem unaware that they've done so. Think of the friend who shows up to a birthday party dinner and fills her plate with bread and salad because she's no longer eating meat. And how you pretend you're interested in the latest book she read or documentary she saw about the treatment of farm animals. You listen, of course, because she's your friend. Then, at your next party, six months later, after you've taken pains to make sure there are vegetarian options available, she puts a hot dog on her plate.

Just like that, she's changed her mind yet again. It's her right to do so, indeed all people's right—and politicians have the right as well.

Flip-flop is a term that is used so often, we've forgotten that it wasn't always a part of the English language.

In 1890, the *New York Times* first used *flip-flop* to refer to a change in a political candidate's opinion. John W. Goff, candidate for district attorney, said of one of his opponents,

I would like to hear Mr. Nicoll explain this great flip-flop, for three years ago, you know, as the Republican candidate for District Attorney, he bitterly denounced Tammany as a party run by bosses and in the interest of bossism ... Nicoll, who three years ago was denouncing Tammany, is its candidate to-day [sic].

Tom Wicker, a *Times* columnist, used the term in 1967 to comment on recent events, and the word seemed to take off from there.

Tom Wicker wrote a *Times* op-ed piece in 1988 citing some classic examples of politicians flip-flopping. Ronald Reagan provided a classic example, a politician who raised taxes and signed a liberal abortion law when he was governor of California. Then, when running for president in 1980, he denounced both tax increases and abortion. Wicker mentioned the many flip-flops of Dick Gephardt, congressional leader for the Democratic Party from 1989 to 2003, ranging from an opposition to abortion and then qualified acceptance of the practice, and from supporting private school tuition tax credits to strong opposition. During his time in politics, Al Gore went from rejecting an oil import tax to a soft yes. He also first supported farm loan production limits, then was outraged by them.

Wicker claims there's actually nothing wrong with flip-flopping—as long as it's done for the right reasons. He notes that the politician doing the flip-flop needs to admit to it. Covering up a change of opinion or stubbornly insisting, "No, I never said that," is considered lying. For an example of an ethical flip-flop, Robert Kennedy once expressed his opposition to the death penalty to a reporter. The journalist, who was obviously well-prepared, replied, "But didn't you use to support the death penalty?" Kennedy answered, "That was before I read [Albert] Camus." During his terms, President Obama admitted to "evolving" on his opinion of gay marriage despite the fact he had spent the prior years in a Christian congregation that sternly rebuked the practice. Admitting to a change of heart while providing a legitimate reason for it is perfectly acceptable.

Wicker explains the three other acceptable forms of flip-flopping. One is for a politician to justify it in terms of personal growth, the desire to keep an open mind. Dick Gephardt once said, "I'd rather change and be right than be rigid and be wrong." In 1960, John F. Kennedy worked to persuade liberals that he had outgrown his tolerance of Senator Joseph R. McCarthy—a flip-flop that was definitely worth making.

When a politician moves from a local stage to the national stage, a flip-flop is often practical, even warranted. Lyndon Johnson opposed most civil rights bills as a senator from Texas. However, when he was president, he pushed through the Civil Rights Act of 1964 and the Voting Rights Act. It's easy to forget that the needs of one particular state are often different from the needs of the federal government, and a smart politician accepts that.

Wicker's final justification for flip-flopping is changed circumstances. One of the most famous flip-flops in history occurred with Richard Nixon. In 1964, he said, "It would be disastrous to the cause of freedom," for the United States to recognize Red China—even though that's precisely what he ended up doing by sending Secretary of State Kissinger on the secret trip to Beijing in 1971. To paraphrase Mao Zedong, you are the one who sees when an opportunity comes and then knows that you must seize the hour and seize the day.

Do Trump's flip-flops land in any of these "acceptable" categories? It's important to look at Trump as a person and at his approach to politics. Most politicians, and in particular presidential candidates, craft detailed focus-group platforms from which to launch their campaigns. They spend years developing and then selling their brand to voters. Trump didn't start his run for president because he'd moved up the ranks politically or gained a following of voters. Instead, he said that his presidential campaign of 2016 was convenient for him because in previous years, he would have needed to break business contracts to make such a run possible. He also said that he started his run because he needed to do it for himself. He didn't want to look back years from now and think *woulda, coulda, shoulda*. This reasoning is a far cry from the reasoning of politicians who've shared the stage with him, and the implications are significant.

Since beginning his campaign, Trump's been faced with questions regarding issues he's never had to seriously consider, mostly because his opinion didn't actually matter until then. He could oppose abortion in a casual manner because his decision didn't affect anybody. Today, Trump realizes that he needs to wrestle with his stances, not just on some issues, but on every issue. The most challenging aspect of such a scenario is that a lot of his "thinking it through" occurs on camera.

ARE YOU A FLIP-FLOPPER?

Imagine you decided to become a teacher, and the first question you were asked at an interview was, "What's your ideology in education? Is it constructivism or behaviorism?" You would do your best to answer and hope those interviewing you understood your response. Now, imagine your interview is on camera for the entire country to watch. You are not a seasoned teacher with years under your belt; you are a newbie hoping to break into the field because you have a lot to offer. If you hesitate, you're criticized. If you say something different from what you wrote on a paper you turned in back in college 10 years ago, it's gleefully pointed out to you. Any variances from opinions expressed in the past, any rethinking or on-the-spot considerations mean that you are pejoratively labeled a "flip-flopper."

Does that make you a poor candidate to be an educator? Of course not. You very well may be more passionate and competent than many candidates who offer pat answers that have not varied year-in and year-out. You may just need some practice and guidance when it comes to interviewing. We could say the same for Trump. The style of his comments and answers, most coming under intense scrutiny, and with countless analysts parsing every syllable, should not be our primary focus. We should reward substance over style. Even Hillary Clinton, the now long-time professional politician, admitted that she had "short-circuited" under the pressure of the questions about her email scandal.

In May, A *Washington Post* article by Daniel W. Drezner points out that Trump views all of his pre-campaign statements as "not really counting." Trump saw himself as an entertainer, not a politician. "I never anticipated running for office or being a politician, so I could have fun with Howard [Stern] on the radio, and everyone would love it. People do love it. I could say whatever I wanted when I was an entrepreneur, a business guy." Trump has no shame when it comes to past behavior or statements because he wasn't trying to "not get caught" in some sort of lie.

The presidential campaign of 2016 has seen perhaps a record number of flip-flops. For example, Bernie Sanders wrote in 1997, "If, by chance, I win the Democratic nomination, I will respectfully decline. I am an independent and proud of it." And yet, we saw how aggressively he sought the Democratic nomination for president, so much so that he almost became a math denier. (Although the Democratic Party primary was not officially over, Hillary Clinton had obtained enough total delegates to win the nomination; at that point, short of her death, she was a lock.) On the other side of the aisle, Ted Cruz said, "Congress needs to strengthen the country's bargaining position by establishing trade-promotion authority, also known as TPA." Two months later, he said,

As a general matter, I agree that free trade is good for America. But TPA in this Congress has become enmeshed in corrupt Washington backroom deal making, along with serious concerns that it would open up the potential for sweeping changes in our laws that trade agreements typically do not include.

This was a glaring contradiction. Marco Rubio co-authored an immigration reform bill in 2013 generally referred to as the "Gang of Eight," which spent money to fortify the U.S.–Mexico border as it offered a pathway to citizenship. In 2014, he said he no longer believes the time is right for a pathway to citizenship. As secretary of state, Hillary Clinton called the Trans-Pacific Partnership the "gold standard in trade agreements." Then, in May 2015, when asked why she had turned noncommittal, she said, "I have said I want to judge the final agreement." That's political speak for *wiggle room*. Yet it is Trump's flip-flops that seem to draw the most ire from political writers.

Columnist Jane C. Timm wrote the article "A Full List of Donald Trump's Rapidly Changing Policy Positions" that focuses on Trump's fluid opinions. Donald Trump said he was pro-choice in 1999 and during the campaign told CNN he is now pro-life. His vacillation goes deeper. He said that states should decide how to handle abortions but followed that by saying women who have abortions should be punished. That same day, he said it should be the doctor who performed the surgery who is legally responsible, making the woman the victim. That leaves us at his current position, which is in favor of banning abortions without criminalizing women who pursue them illegally.

Trump's stand on immigration has also seen some modifications. Initially, he said that he wanted to build a wall and deport all 11 million undocumented immigrants. Then he migrated to a softer stance: let's deport the undocumented immigrants and then bring the "good" ones back legally. He noted that the illegal immigrants "who were brought to the United States as children, who have lived and gone to school here, and who in many cases identify as American" (Dreamers) might be able to stay—then quickly changed his mind, retracting that statement. As far as the public remembers, Trump still wants to deport illegal immigrants, including the Dreamers. However, in off-the-record talks with the *New York Times*, Trump intimated he might be flexible with this stance. He continues to refuse to release the transcript of this conversation.

In August of 2015, Trump stated his intention to repeal Obamacare completely. Then he added that, even though he had vowed to repeal the legislation, he said that he wants everyone covered and that the mandate was a good idea. Later, he claimed that not everyone would be covered.

You get the point: Trump changes his mind, *a lot*. He has most likely committed the biggest number of flip-flops in 2016's campaign. Why does Trump appear so wishy-washy on such pressing issues? There are many factors to consider.

What the American people need to focus on is not the fact that Trump flip-flops but *whether his flip-flopping will be in the best interest of the electorate* once he assumes the presidency. If Trump is able to be pragmatic, to focus on solutions rather than party doctrine, if changing his mind means he will be willing to flip-flop in the name of getting things done and moving forward, ideology be damned, that represents not just a step toward a refreshing change in political style for this county but a giant leap forward in leadership. Trump would be a rare president, not leading just with words to drum up the base but with effective action to call a nation together. In reality, we need to hope Trump continues to flip-flop, or, more correctly stated, we need to hope Donald Trump continues to have an open mind not tied to symbols related to elephants and donkeys. Jamelle Bouie wrote an article for Slate.com titled "Our Best Presidents Are Flip-Floppers" in which he details how the most successful presidents have changed their minds throughout their political careers. When Abraham Lincoln took office in 1861, he was moderate on slavery and opposed immediate abolition. By his second term, however, Lincoln had embraced black soldiers, floated the idea of black voting rights, and issued the Emancipation Proclamation. He adjusted on the fly and was a better president for it.

Woodrow Wilson changed his stance on the decision to enter World War I. His 1916 re-election platform was centered on a notion that he would keep the United States out of war; a year later, American troops were in Europe. In fact, it was our involvement that broke the stalemate and helped end the catastrophic World War I—this Great War had claimed millions of European lives. Even Ronald Reagan reversed his decision to negotiate with the Soviets about arms control and nuclear disarmament.

The moral here is simple: the more we learn, the more we change. Upon consideration, today's absolute belief may become tomorrow's cast-aside idea, an intellectual dead end. Instead of criticizing flip-flopping, we should see it as a skill. Some of the greatest presidential decisions were often ones that defied what a leader had said in the past or what his political advisers recommended or what conventional wisdom seemed to support. The best presidents, in fact, use it to further their goals or take advantage of a new opportunity. What we don't need or want is a rigid president who is unwilling to listen and prioritize the needs of the people.

The Trump campaign itself is a study in the prudent flip-flop. Trump has not denied it himself. He has just begun to understand that his message of substance and truth was getting lost behind harsh and brash words, which, admittedly, may have resonated and activated those of us who are hurting and who feel left out of the system. It made him great and successful with some but turned off those who are not used to the New York style.

Trump seems proud to change his campaign and his mind, not pivoting but growing, and he can't hide his resentment when he gets a question he doesn't like, unlike most politicians, who have no issues with sporting a pasted-on smile as they dive into a canned answer. Trump may answer, but when he thinks the question is stupid, he can't seem to pretend otherwise just to please some political writer. Should not that kind of behavior be encouraged and rewarded? When so many Americans lament that lying politicians will say anything to get a vote, can't they then see the wisdom of supporting someone who refuses to practice what they preach against?

A lot can be gleaned from Trump's tone, and he seems unable to be disingenuous. It's fairly easy to tell when Trump is saying something but not really meaning it, but that doesn't happen often, and those who distrust the mainstream media see this as a strength of Trump's: *he's unwilling to play the game.* Ultimately, Trump's obvious sincerity may matter more than the beauty of his phrasing, and if his transparency of character means more flip-flopping than the average professional politician may display, then hallelujah for that.

And whatever happened to Trump Airlines? How about Trump University? And then there's Trump Magazine and Trump Vodka and Trump Steaks and Trump Mortgage.

—GOVERNOR MITT ROMNEY

CHAPTER 8

PLANES, STEAK, & WATER

IN THE 1950S, a University of Wisconsin student, Joanne, dated a Syrian student for a short time and unfortunately found herself pregnant. The baby was born in San Francisco, and Joanne immediately put him up for adoption. She chose a couple who promised that the boy would attend college after high school; this promise was her main criteria for choosing her son's adoptive parents.

The adopted father restored cars as a hobby and set up a workbench for the boy when he was old enough to learn the trade. The boy's new mother taught him to read before he reached kindergarten—another activity he loved. Like many kids with exceptional intellectual abilities, the boy had a difficult time making friends.

As promised, the boy enrolled in college, but he dropped out when a friend found him a job at Atari, the early computer console company. A few months later, in the early 1970s, he left the company and spent several months in India, visiting ashrams and simply drifting. He would seek out free food wherever he could find it and meditate throughout his evenings. When he returned home, he dove into the psychedelic scene of Northern California. He soon realized that he was a failure—he had failed at school, at work, even at Buddhism. It seemed that there was no place for him, nothing he could stick to, and nothing at which he would excel. Desperately needing a job, he was surprised when Atari agreed to take him back. Apparently, he had impressed them during his short tenure, months before.

That was when the light bulb blinked on above his head. This intelligent but wandering "failure" realized that he had the vision, the marketing sense, and the foresight to beat the big computer companies at their own game. So he founded a new computer company in his garage and named it Apple Computer.

This college dropout and free spirit was, of course, Steve Jobs, one of the most successful American businesspeople of modern times. The friend who helped him find the job at Atari was Steve Wozniak. In 1976, the duo created the first Apple home computer, which debuted at the West Coast Computer Fair and set Jobs on the path to becoming a millionaire just a few years later, when he was 23 years old.

Failure led to success, as it does in life and business, at least for those of us wise enough to learn and profit from our failures. "Failures" pave the path to our successes, from the time we first struggle to walk upright and fall on our rumps, to the first time we swing a baseball bat and miss the ball by a mile, to the countless times when employers tell us we "just aren't right for the job." Failure is a vital part of the human experience because the only way to achieve great things is to put yourself and your work out there for judgment by others. Criticism can be harsh, early successes are rare, and a person's efforts often seem futile, a waste of time. At that point, many of us fold and quit, or pursue more modest goals. The most successful among us shrug, accept the result, learn a lesson, and press on, regardless. They realize that the greatest hitters in baseball often set records for strike-outs. They know that they need to try different strategies and techniques until they get it right. They know that the only sure way *not* to fail is not to try.

Trump has such a mindset. Critics point to his handful of business failures, particularly the bankruptcies of some of his subsidiaries, as a reason he won't succeed as president. What they fail to realize is that these failures—and the successes that followed—make him a uniquely qualified candidate.

Hillary Clinton, with no business experience or entrepreneurial success whatsoever, demonizes Trump on this issue, conveniently ignoring the fact that Trump's business successes have been myriad, his failures few (and many of those beyond his influence or control), and his place as a titan of modern business is secure.

In the true spirit of Donald Trump, let's dive headfirst into a no-holds-barred examination his so-called failures.

Trump Airlines took flight when Trump spent $365 million for Eastern Air Shuttle, a service that had been running hourly flights between Boston, New York City, and Washington D.C. for 27 years. With the deal, he acquired 17 Boeing 727s, plus landing strips and facilities at each of the shuttle's stopovers. He wanted to transform a simple business into a luxury experience by adding wood floors, chrome seat-belt latches, and gold-plated bathroom fixtures.

As it turned out, customers had apparently valued the shuttle service for its convenience, and most seemed uninterested in a "luxury" experience. At the same time, fuel prices rose significantly with the start of the Gulf War in 1990. The combination proved deadly to Trump's vision. Trump was just too far ahead of his time.

A more recent failure occurred in 2007 with Trump Steaks. He joined forces with Sharper Image and QVC to "deliver a taste of Donald Trump's luxurious lifestyle." His on-air pitch: "Trump Steaks are by far the best-tasting, most flavorful beef you've ever had. Truly in a league of their own." Behind Trump were stacked black boxes with *Trump Steaks* in gold lettering. After all, the Trump brand was masculine, decadent, upscale. The product seemed a perfect fit for his brand.

The Sharper Image–Trump partnership was a little odd, though. Sharper Image is known for electronics, not food, gourmet or otherwise. They struggled to expand their image accordingly and unify it with the Trump Steak brand, featuring Trump on the front of their magazine and placing huge posters of Trump in the windows of almost 200 stores nationwide.

Sales never left the ground, though the Sharper Image's business picked up, presumably from customers wandering into the stores to see why Donald Trump's face was in the window. After two short months, Sharper Image pulled the steaks from their shelves. Was this merger with Sharper Image too farfetched? Possibly. Were the steaks simply not good? Also possible. It's difficult to say what made Trump Steaks such a poor seller, but they are officially off the market and have been for some time. Trump Steaks were products, and from New Coke to Windows 8, products sometimes don't resonate with the public. That's the way it goes.

In 2004, the first season of *The Apprentice* aired. The show featured contestants who were judged by their business decisions in various contexts. In one episode, players were split into two teams and charged with selling Trump Ice on the streets of New York City. The bottled water featured Donald Trump's face on the label along with the tagline, "Trump Ice Natural Spring Water is one of the highest quality spring waters bottled in the world with an optimal mineral content. It is bottled in a modern facility and continually tested." The winning team on *The Apprentice* brought in more than $6,000.

Afterward, Trump Ice was distributed to grocery stores and

specialty food stores throughout the United States. According to Trump's 2015 Financial Disclosure Form, his personal earnings from Trump Ice in 2014 was $280,000. According to the Trump website, the only place to find Trump Ice today is at his hotels, restaurants, and golf clubs.

And then there was Trump Vodka, another unsuccessful product. The label announced *Success Distilled*, and the advertising campaign claimed the product would "demand the same respect and inspire the same awe as the international legacy and brand of Donald Trump himself." Trump crossed his fingers that the T&T, or Trump and tonic, would become the most ordered drink in the country. When featured on *Larry King Live*, Trump said he jumped into the vodka business to outdo his friends at Grey Goose. Once again, his new product generated little interest, and the company stopped production in 2011. Today, Trump and his team seem to realize that his brand does not translate well to consumer products. That's the way it goes. On to the next venture.

Of course, most critics bring up Trump Plaza Hotel and Casino in Atlantic City. But to be fair, Atlantic City—once thought to be a gold mine by gaming concerns—has in fact turned into somewhat of a casino graveyard. The great Steve Wynn, frustrated by New Jersey officials who seemed intent on destroying the promise that Atlantic City held, bailed from Atlantic City years ago, claiming that the local government was "corrupt and stupid." Revel, a $2.4 billion casino, opened in 2012, then closed its doors in 2014. Florida developer Glenn Straub bought the casino in 2015, with plans to reopen, but months later announced that he would likely abandon the casino before it opens. Straub said, "This state stinks. It just stinks … I worked in five states. This is 10 times worse than what it would be anyplace else." In 2014, the Center for Gaming Research reported that Atlantic City's casino revenues had fallen more than 45 percent since 2006. Clearly, even the most audacious and determined developers have found that it's tough to keep a business alive in Atlantic City.

Trump: The Game, Trump University, GoTrump.com—there are others—failed to reach orbit. Trump has explained his failures on a number of occasions: "Part of being a winner is knowing when enough is enough. Sometimes you have to give up the fight and walk away, and move on to something that's more productive."

There have been many times that Trump has walked away from an investment because it wasn't going anywhere. Why keep trying to pound a square peg into a round hole? Trump can also feel confident in the way he reacts to his failures. Think about the last time you threw in all your chips, invested time or money or both, and the project failed. Certainly, that feeling stings, but Trump doesn't allow his failed ventures to define him. Instead, he looks forward to his next possible success.

FAR MORE SUCCESSES THAN FAILURES

Now, let's take a look at some of Trump's many successes.

In 1974, Trump bought the former Commodore Hotel in New York City from Penn Central Railroad. The Bowman-Biltmore Hotels group built the hotel in 1919 and named it after "Commodore" Cornelius Vanderbilt. The lobby has been called the "Most Beautiful Lobby in the World" and was the single largest room in the hotel. The Commodore was successful for decades, but by the late 1970s, the Penn Central railroad line was decaying and unprofitable, and the hotel no longer in fashion. The railroad went bankrupt, and Trump immediately took advantage of a golden opportunity, one that, considering its pitfalls and complications, would have frightened off many less determined entrepreneurs.

It was one of Trump's first major construction projects in Manhattan. He completely rebuilt and modernized the building, gutting the first few floors down to steel frames. The only part of the décor that wasn't touched was the foyer to the grand ballroom; he wisely chose to retain its neoclassical columns and plasterwork. The hotel reopened as the Grand Hyatt New York, with entrances to the Park Avenue Viaduct and to 42nd Street. Trump's hotel won the 2007 and 2008 *Corporate and Incentive Travel* magazine Award of Excellence. The hotel still booms today.

Trump's next project, just a little farther north in Manhattan, was Trump Tower, a mixed-use skyscraper located on Fifth Avenue in Midtown. The Tower is not only the headquarters for the Trump Organization but also Donald Trump's personal residence. At 48 stories, the tower features highly sought-after residential real estate. People who live or have lived there include Bruce Willis, Cristiano Ronaldo, and Andrew Lloyd-Webber.

Another New York City landmark is Wollman Rink, the public ice rink in the southern half of Central Park. It opened in 1949 and would stay open through the summer months as a concert venue, hosting the likes of Led Zeppelin, the Allman Brothers, Tammy Wynette, Peggy Lee, Judy Collins, and Pete Seeger. Today, it features the Victorian Gardens Amusement Park. In 1980, the rink closed for a proposed two-years' worth of renovations, projected at some $9.1 million a year. By 1986, the project still wasn't finished and had cost $13 million. It was Donald Trump who persuaded then-Mayor Ed Koch to let him complete the work in four months at $2.5 million and open the place by the end of the year. Trump's stipulations were that he be allowed to run the venue and an adjacent restaurant where he could use the profits to recoup the costs he'd laid down for the project. The mayor resisted, but eventually caved, most likely from embarrassment, and the project was completed. Wollman Rink is now known as the Trump Skating Rink. Without Trump, who knows how long the rink would have languished, mired in cost overruns and red tape?

Another of Trump's great successes is his NBC show *The Apprentice*. Trump hosted the show and also served as the executive producer, raking in $1 million per episode. The show did well enough that it inspired a spin-off aptly called *The Celebrity Apprentice*, which is still cranking out new seasons, even though Trump no longer appears on any of the programs.

New York City isn't the only city where Trump's successes are evident. In 2005, Trump purchased the former *Chicago Sun-Times* headquarters for $73 million and converted it into the Trump International Hotel and Tower, the second-tallest building in Chicago. Within its walls are housed a hotel, condos, restaurants, and upscale shops. It was named *Travel+Leisure's* best large city hotel in North America in 2010.

The sheer number of his pursuits is extraordinary. Ultimately, Trump has his hand in a large number of pots. He is notorious for taking huge risks and using a large amount of start-up capital to do so. Is such risk-taking a good characteristic of someone who wants to be president of the United States?

Before you answer, consider the following.

In a podcast from Knowledge@Wharton, presidential historian Richard Norton Smith offered 10 rules for presidential evaluations that stand the test of time. The first was simple: *History rewards the risk-takers.*

When bold initiatives were pushed through, the rewards were great. Thomas Jefferson made the Louisiana Purchase even though it ran counter to his party's principles and, most likely, was unconstitutional. Harry Truman stopped communist aggression in Korea by deploying troops even though World War II had barely concluded. Lyndon Johnson passed the Civil Rights Act of 1964 despite the carnage that he knew it would cause his own party.

The poster child for presidential risk-taking (with a boldness that some thought approached arrogance) could be Teddy Roosevelt, who broke up monopolies and developed the Square Deal. He promoted the conservation movement to preserve America's natural resources, passed the Meat Inspection Act, and signed the Pure Food and Drug Act to regulate food production. His foreign policy accomplishments included issuing a corollary to the Monroe Doctrine, negotiating U.S. control of construction of the Panama Canal, and negotiating an end to the Russo-Japanese War, for which he won a Nobel Prize.

Most historians have written about Roosevelt's accomplishments in a way that ranks him among the greatest of all American presidents. However, many of his contemporaries didn't feel that way. Mark Twain wrote, "Theodore Roosevelt is one of the most impulsive men in existence … He flies from one thing to another with incredible dispatch—throws a somersault and is straightaway back again where he was last week. He will then throw some more somersaults, and nobody can foretell where he is finally going to land after the series. Each act of his, and each opinion expressed, is likely to abolish or convert some previous act or expressed opinion. That is what is happening to him all the time as president." Hmm, does this sound like someone you know?

People's disdain for Donald Trump sounds awfully similar to Mark Twain's sentiment about Roosevelt. Is it possible that Trump could be the new Roosevelt? In a *Forbes* article written by TR descendent Dr. Theodore Roosevelt Malloch, the erstwhile president is described as wanting America to thrive again in its full glory. Malloch makes the parallel clear: "Trump realizes what we have lost in Obamanation and calls it the abomination that it is. The country wants to find its rightful place again, and this is why Trump resonates, not just with Republicans but also with Reagan Democrats and even the trade unions. He resonates with every aspiring soul who wants the freedom to be what America always was—a beacon of hope and a land of opportunity"; indeed, that "shining city on a hill."

A plague is sweeping the land, gathering victims of all shapes and sizes and turning them into fools. Its name— for now—is Trumpism.

—CHARLES C.W. COOKE

CHAPTER 9

KEVIN WILLIAMSON

DEPAUW UNIVERSITY IS a small, private liberal arts school located in the middle of the dusty cornfields in Greencastle, Indiana. *US News* ranked the university number 51 in its list of Best National Liberal Arts Colleges. Widely known for its spirited student body and Greek life, DePauw is home to the nation's first Kappa Alpha Theta and Alpha Chi Omega sorority chapters. *The Princeton Review* has ranked DePauw number one in Greek life at American colleges numerous times over the last 15 years.

In the fall of 2006, national representatives from the Delta Zeta sorority arrived on DePauw's campus to interview its active sorority members. The national officers were concerned by the chapter's declining membership, and the sorority higher-ups had come to weed out those not actively participating in the house. Just before final exams that semester, 35 Delta Zeta sisters were told to resign on the grounds that they were insufficiently committed to recruitment and the sorority as a whole. The 12 women who remained members of Delta Zeta had one obvious thing in common: they were conventionally attractive. The national chapter had sent a clear message: *This is what a sorority girl is supposed to look like.*

Most overweight or minority members had been summarily dismissed. Even the chapter's president was booted out. Feeling discouraged and isolated, some of the dismissed Delta Zeta sisters simply dropped out of school. However, it did not take them long to put the pieces together and recognize the true reasons for their dismissal. Some of the women who remained quit in protest. Non-member students rallied, parents and alumni wrote letters, and a faculty petition was drawn up, denouncing the sorority's actions as elitist and unethical. In March of the following year, the president of DePauw rescinded Delta Zeta's charter as a recognized campus organization, stating that the national organization's values were not compatible with those of the university.

Of course, the women of Delta Zeta national should judge their members on their core principles and values rather than on their outward appearances. They should have asked, "What can she bring to the table?" as opposed to thinking, "I can judge her at a glance."

We have been witnessing the same elitist pooh-poohing within the Republican establishment when they consider presidential candidate Donald Trump.

The "Republican establishment" refers to the permanent political class and structure that constitutes the party's leadership and typically controls the rules, elections, and funding disbursements within the Republican Party. In general, establishment Republican politicians have appeased their base with talk of fiscal conservatism while remaining moderate-to-liberal in their voting on issues regarding the size and scope of government. Since the end of the Reagan era (and more accurately, it might have even started with Nixon), George H.W. Bush, Bob Dole, John McCain, Lindsay Graham, John Boehner, Arlen Specter, Jon Huntsman, Charlie Crist, and Susan Collins have been the principal actors atop the Republican hierarchy. Unfortunately, these Republicans have largely ignored their oaths to defend the Constitution and to practice fiscal conservatism. Instead, their loyalty has been to special interest groups, and they each spent like drunken sailors while ballooning the national debt. On the other end of the spectrum are "conservative Republicans," who often come from the party's grassroots. These are quixotic politicians who honor their pledges. They tend to be the newer faces in Washington, such as Iowa's Joni Ernst or Texas Senator Ted Cruz. Of this group, the chief antagonists of the Republican establishment have been Sarah Palin and South Carolina Senator Jim DeMint. In past elections, Palin's endorsements buoyed some candidates to underdog wins against presumptive establishment nominees. Palin explicitly described this intraparty conflict in a 2012 Facebook post: "The Republican establishment, which fought Ronald Reagan in the 1970s and which continues to fight the grassroots Tea Party movement today, has adopted the tactics of the left in using the media and the politics of personal destruction to attack an opponent."

Donald Trump is not part of the GOP establishment, nor should he be considered a member of any grassroots Republican group such as the Tea Party. Trump is synonymous with the non-modelesque girl who shows up to rush a sorority, speaking a little too loudly and asking for an extra brownie. Sorority girls, like the Republican candidate running for President, are expected to behave in a certain way. When Donald Trump announced his bid for the presidency, the GOP did not make an effort to understand him because he did not fit their mold—he neither looked nor acted the part. He did not fit in.

The blowback was immediate and intense. Out of the gate, Kevin Williamson wrote an article titled, "Witless Ape Rides Escalator," in which he mocked Trump's candidacy, called his father a slumlord, attacked his wife, and compared him to a baboon. Williamson went on to detail Trump's lack of policy substance. He concluded the piece with the suggestion that we ought to crucify Trump and see if he rises from the dead like the Christ-like figure he thinks he is.

This article was published on June 16, 2015 at 4:30 pm, which is significant because it was only a few hours after Trump announced his candidacy. He was never given a chance. He walked into Delta Zeta, and the popular girls decided he was too damned *different to* represent their brand.

Williamson did not stop there. In another article written on March 28, 2016, he took aim at Trump's supporters. The vitriol is breathtaking:

The truth about these dysfunctional, downscale communities is that they deserve to die. Economically, they are negative assets. Morally, they are indefensible. Forget all your cheap theatrical Bruce Springsteen crap. Forget your sanctimony about struggling Rust Belt factory towns and your conspiracy theories about the wily Orientals stealing our jobs.... The white American underclass is in thrall to a vicious, selfish culture whose main products are misery and used heroin needles. Donald Trump's speeches make them feel good. So does OxyContin. What they need isn't analgesics, literal or political. They need real opportunity, which means that they need real change, which means that they need U-Haul.

For Kevin Williamson, it appears that access to the proper schools, speaking with correct syntax, and understanding the difference between "their" and "there" should be the prerequisites for voting. In the midst of exercising his own rights, Williamson seemingly forgot that the single most beautiful thing about our country is that everyone has a right to his or her opinion—and the right to express that opinion in the voting booth. The tone of his article was that of a schoolyard bully belittling others as geeks and fatsos. He made readers feel as though they would have to be witless to vote for this man. This says more about

Kevin Williamson than it does about Trump or his supporters. While he seemingly supported a government of the people for years, Williamson is apparently more comfortable with roving correspondents than with housekeepers or postal workers. Respect for Williamson notwithstanding, in truth, it was his own witlessness and that of the Republican establishment to miss the fact that billionaire Donald Trump could be the man to bridge the gap between the GOP and the African-American and lower-income communities; or that Donald Trump might be able to use his celebrity status to bring fiscally conservative values into the mainstream through his Hollywood connections—something the Democratic Party does with quite a bit of success. Instead, Williamson perpetuated the divide, making it clear that the smug, upper-class, white elite have the luxury of looking down on the working class—regardless of their race.

Sorry, Mr. Williamson. This is a democracy, and all votes count equally.

Williamson's article was meant to strike fear into people for thinking of Trump as a legitimate contender. It also seemed intended to shame. Williamson is not the only Republican taking such a stance, and these actions beg the question—*what is everyone so afraid of?* Of course, Trump is different and unconventional, but why the intense backlash? Why has he rattled so many Republicans? The most likely answer is that there is fear among the establishment that they will not be able to control Trump or the system. Say what you will about Trump, but he is nobody's puppet.

Part of Donald Trump's brand is his willpower. The Republican establishment, somewhat unintelligently, sees this as his tragic flaw, refusing to acknowledge that Trump has spun gold time and time again. True, his father lent him a million dollars, but he turned that into a few *billion* dollars, whereas many others in similar situations have chosen to get high and live off Daddy's money for as long as possible. There was a time when many in the elite Manhattan circles mocked Trump, but they soon found themselves outsmarted and outmaneuvered by this vocal upstart. This year, millions of voters have proven that he is no joke as a politician, either.

These kneejerk, hysterical attacks on Trump are part of a game that could prove lethal to the GOP and the American electorate in general. Shortsighted bullies such as Mr. Williamson may not be fully aware of how risky their words have been to the Republican Party, but there are some important voter groups who are fully aware of Williamson's poisoned message. Certainly, African-Americans read his articles and hear the "I'm better than you" subtext that should be the sole domain of the elitist left. Other non-elites, such as members of the LGBT community and working-class women, often recognize Williamson's attitude for what it is.

Still clueless about the long-term impact of his rhetoric, Williamson was recently quoted as saying, "My own attitude toward the Republican Party has been for some time like Winston Churchill's attitude toward the Church of England: not a pillar by any means but a buttress, supporting it from the outside."

We need to stop wasting time questioning whether Trump is a "real conservative." The definition of a conservative has been so altered over the years that it has lost all real meaning. So-called "conservatives" have proven themselves to be no different than free-spending progressives, and that is a problem. Republican voters now know that George W. Bush grossly expanded the role of the federal government and racked up eye-popping deficits, which pretty much aligns with the "strategy" of Obama and the Democrats. Social benefits are a one-way street; once people get a taste of government handouts, they will not give up those benefits. In other words, those who are concerned that Trump will make the GOP lose its way must not have been paying attention. The party has been lost for some time. Trump was not, and will not be, the death of the Republican Party. Trump is *the result of* the death of the GOP. He is a conservative, albeit a new type of conservative. Considering the breadth of support he has found among the American people, it would seem that the GOP would find some common ground and embrace him, but instead he has been rejected in a short-sighted attempt to shoehorn the usual gang of party automatons into the election process.

Robert Kagan has a better idea of what has been building over the last few years: "Let's be clear: Trump is no fluke. Nor is he hijacking the Republican Party or the conservative movement, if there is such a thing. He is, rather, the party's creation, its Frankenstein's monster, brought to life by the party, fed by the party, and now made strong enough to destroy its maker."

It is important to consider young Americans, the Millennials and those even younger, who are the future of our country and are playing a large role in fundamentally updating the Republican Party. Key demographics in areas like religion and race are shifting, trends that were put into motion long before Donald Trump came onto the scene.

Consider organized religion. A recent review of surveys conducted over the last 50 years of more than 11 million adolescents shows that Millennials are much less interested than past generations in organized religion. A 2010 Pew survey suggested that people may consider religion more important as they become older, and a 2014 survey found that Millennials do have a strong faith in God, although they identify less with organized religion.

Studies have indicated that individualism among Millennials is high—which often means that religious involvement is low.

Individualism can conflict with religion; organized religions require following certain rules and being part of a homogenous group.

When gay marriage was legalized, the majority of Republicans viewed this change through the lens of organized religion. They lamented that the Supreme Court was compromising the centuries-old definition of marriage (and that the Founding Fathers did not want the judicial branch to legislate from the bench). To Millennials, Republicans did not sound like people concerned about the direction of their party. Instead, the old guard seemed more concerned with legislating sexual choices, and this trajectory is causing the party to lose ground with younger voters. Millennials simply do not relate to many of the current GOP social positions. Modern culture demands that the party move toward the center on social issues. "Millennials have matured quite a bit since 2008 and are no longer the young idealistic generation they once were. They have clawed their way through the poor economy throughout the past eight years, doing everything they can to survive high unemployment numbers, massive student loan debt, Obamacare, and soaring costs of living" (Salvatore La Mastra, *The Blaze).*

The Republican establishment claims that Trump's "temperament" is unsettling; that may be the GOP establishment's coded term for "same old same old." In other words, they know Trump will not feel beholden, either by ambition or by special interest groups, to "pretty up" old ideas and sell them to the American public, and Trump's get-it-done attitude simply frightens them and their financial backers.

The establishment will revolt against anything that is different, anything that forces them to think outside their pocketbook. If it disrupts the status quo, or may erode their power, politicians fear it. It doesn't matter how bipartisan a policy proposal or idea may be. It does not matter how good it may be for the country.

Take, for example, a tax overhaul plan known as the Fair Tax. Unlike the establishment, Trump is not afraid of big ideas. He knows that the present income tax/payroll tax system is failing. And, he knows how Washington works. Mike Huckabee, one of his top advisors and a spokesman, made the Fair Tax legislation the centerpiece of his 2008 and his 2016 presidential campaigns. Mike Pence, his vice-presidential candidate, was a cosponsor of the Fair Tax legislation while a member of the House of Representatives. Both worked closely with Americans For Fair Taxation, the largest tax reform group in the country. Trump needs to do something groundbreaking and "huge" once elected, something that aligns with his oversized personality, and he may find that idea in the Fair Tax plan.

This plan, which has been introduced in every session of Congress since 1994, would reposition our tax base from an income tax/payroll tax system to a system that, like 45 states, taxes retail consumption. Admittedly, this plan does offer radical change, and it requires a paradigm shift regarding how we think about raising revenue. Nevertheless, it has languished—mired in classic gridlock—despite the whispers from behind closed doors that quite a few high-ranking Democrats embrace it and the fact that, in public, many Republicans (73) and six Senate co-sponsors are interested in the Fair Tax.

The Fair Tax plan is one of, if not *the*, oldest and most co-sponsored piece of tax reform in the United States Congress since 1986.

Yet the current establishment, the powers that be, are closed-minded to the opportunities for the real and productive tax reform that the Fair Tax promises, or worse, they simply feel this groundbreaking legislation would be counter to their personal political ambitions, rejecting the idea outright in favor of questionable tax loopholes, over 70,000 pages of tax code, and more importantly, incentives for their special interests.

It is also very frightening for a politician if, as would be true with the Fair Tax, the taxes now hidden from people would be clear. In fact, everyone in the U.S. may not be a wage earner, but they are consumers and each time they make a purchase, they will see the costs of the U.S. government. These consumers will demand that taxes be reduced and this is very troubling to the leaders of both parties—but not to Trump. He knows that people can spend their money much better than government.

Trump has been routinely criticized that his trade proposals, if enacted, could start a trade war that may ultimately hurt the U.S.; however, the establishment is quite aware that the Fair Tax could avoid such a trade war by leveling the playing field for foreign trade. In fact, this new system actually rewards companies that export goods because there is no U.S. tax on U.S. exports but, unlike today, all imports are subject to the Fair Tax. This reverses the present tax policy, which punishes companies that produce exports in the U.S. and rewards companies that move jobs overseas. The best news is that this change won't start a trade war—it is simply a tax system similar to those used by all of our trading partners.

Trump understands all too well that the rapidly growing tax evasion problem, estimated to now exceed $600 billion per year, will get worse as we move from an employee/employer economy, with withholding, to a freelance economy. Many people have elected to not pay taxes on some of their income, and others are filing incorrect tax returns because of honest mistakes. The result is the same—higher and higher rates of tax evasion. Since within the next decade, it is likely that 40 percent of the economy will be freelance, there is likely going to be even more tax evasion. The Fair Tax will have a much lower evasion rate because over 90 percent of the retail sales in the U.S. are made by less than 10 percent of the merchants.

Ultimately, Trump identifies with small business, and nothing would give the true startup (as opposed to the venture capital-based startup) true equality with the big establishment business like getting rid of income and payroll taxes. Big businesses can spend $1 million to $2 million a month hiring the best lawyers, accountants, and cheats in the Beltway to minimize their tax liability, but your local diner can't afford such clever and expensive help with its tax burden.

Think about it this way: A tax reform bill with scores of public supporters in the House and Senate (and even more behind closed doors) has been vetted, tested, and has dozens of compelling whitepapers published in support of it, yet it can't get a fair hearing or be brought to vote. What does that tell us about our political process and the old-boy network behind it? It should tell us that we need to seek forward-thinking candidates who are more concerned with positive change than with their own long-term political careers.

As Trump said, "It's time for some different thinking…" Trump is already surrounding himself with people that are thinking differently and have done so in the past. The Fair Tax would be a brave way to put the substantial talents of these people to use for his administration, and for the country.

If the establishment and their surrogates such as Kevin Williamson (who, surprise, has had occasion to disparage Fair Tax supporters) had not so blindly opposed Trump and instead given him a shot, they might have had a better chance to influence his campaign and his policy, be it his attitude toward the Fair Tax, his blunt speaking manner, or his views about social issues. If the GOP has any sort of future, the arrogant, unyielding attitude of the party's elders and their writing surrogates such as Bill Kristol need to change—quickly. Or people will continue to feel that there is no hope left or no way for them to succeed without government, then the wealthy and generous America that the world has come to know and rely on will largely cease to exist. Establishment Republicans failed to generate any voter excitement about any single candidate until Donald Trump tossed his hat into the ring, and no one else in the current crop of presidential contenders seems able to grab the voter's attention like Donald Trump.

Imagine this: President Trump creates an economic resurgence through not only renewed consumer confidence and sound free-market stimulus but, also, through tangible widely supported policies, which return education powers to the states, drastically change Obamacare into something that works and brings about massive tax reform change. Picture more money in your pockets, less government debt, and a balanced budget. In such a scenario, we might be able to swing back to true fiscal conservatism. But, if that is just too much for your cranium, simply picture the head explosions of every beltway establishment politician when they utter the words, President Trump.

What the Hell Do You Have to Lose?

—DONALD TRUMP

ACKNOWLEDGEMENTS

If I could speak to the ether, I would tell those who are venturing on their journey to this planet that absolutely nothing can prepare you for life. There is no amount of training or schooling that will ever prepare you for the first time you fall in love or the first time you break up, the feeling you get when you receive your first paycheck, and the rage you feel after you lose that first job. There is nothing that can prepare you for failure, and likewise, there is nothing to teach you success. The fact that you are not prepared does not mean you are alone.

Thank you for your inspiration and support!

Bran'Di, Bri'An, and
Britt'Ni Davis
The Banks Family
Steve Hayes
Scott Hogenson
Mandi Sadler
Frederick Mooney
The Cohen Family
K.J. Hodge
John Ford
Adina Graham
Dr. Andrew Grossman

Cindy Canevaro
My Editor ~ K. J. Sheldon
The Jackson Family
The Ashley Family
Henry Caruthers
Ozella Lawrence
The Stegall Family
The Davis Family
Jack Grubman
Karen Schoen
Lauren Toland
Alberta DeWalt

NOTES/SOURCES

Citations may apply to multiple chapters. In an effort to simplify, each citation is therefore only listed in one location.

CHAPTER I

"The Dividing of America." *The Economist.* Jul 16, 2016.

"The Fifth Stage of Grief." *The Economist.* May 7, 2016.

"Trump Triumph." *The Economist.* May 7, 2016.

Altman, Alex. "Tribal Warrior." *Time Magazine.* Mar 14, 2016.

Miller, Zeke J. "A Convention Unlike Any Other: Can the GOP Hold It Together?" *Time Magazine.* Jul 25, 2016.

Von Drehle, David. "The Art of the Steal." *Time Magazine.* Jan 18, 2016.

Hook. "As Party Reels, Pence Backs Ryan After Trump's Snub." *The Wall Street Journal.* Aug 4, 2016

http://www.cnn.com/2015/06/26/
politics/2016-candidates-gay-marriage-supreme-court/

http://www.edweek.org/ew/section/multimedia/no-child-left-behind-overview-definition-summary.html

http://www.freerepublic.com/focus/f-chat/3423672/posts

http://www.huffingtonpost.com/2015/05/27/millennials-less-religious_n_7452998.html

http://www.nationalinterest.org/feature/
trumps-speech-signalled-the-end-era-the-gop-17077

http://www.politico.com/magazine/story/2015/07/
republicans-gay-marriage-angry-119711

http://www.politico.com/magazine/story/2016/05/2016-donald-trump-hillary-clinton-election-things-you-should-know-213875

http://www.politico.com/story/2016/06/
apple-wont-aid-gop-convention-over-trump-224513

http://www.rollingstone.com/politics/news/
secret-and-lies-of-the-bailout-20130104

http://www.theatlantic.com/magazine/archive/2016/07/
how-american-politics-went-insane/485570/

http://www.theatlantic.com/magazine/archive/2016/09/
trumps-intellectuals/492752/

http://www.theblaze.com/contributions/
donald-trump-his-rising-poll-numbers-and-millennials/

http://www.usatoday.com/story/news/politics/onpolitics/2016/07/24/
michael-bloomberg-democratic-convention-clinton/87506396/

https://www.washingtonpost.com/news/wonk/wp/2016/07/22/
ivanka-trump-spoke-like-a-democrat-and-republicans-absolutely-loved-it/

CHAPTER 2

Schweizer, Peter. *Clinton Cash: The Untold Story of How and Why Foreign Governments and Businesses Helped Make Bill and Hillary Rich.* New York: HarperCollins, 2015.

Alter, Charlotte. "What Do Women Want?" *Time Magazine.* Aug 1, 2016.

Altman, Alex. "The Apprentices." *Time Magazine.* Jul 25, 2016.

Elliot, Philip. "The Hardest One To Know." *Time Magazine.* Aug 1, 2016.

http://abcnews.go.com/Politics/trump-kids-
meet-gop-candidate-donald-trumps-children/
story?id=35253768

http://time.com/3988288/republican-debate-megyn-kelly/

http://www.bbc.com/news/correspondents/kattykay

http://www.bbc.com/news/world-us-canada-35912640

http://www.businessinsider.com/
hillary-clinton-is-piling-up-endorsements-from-rappers-2015-5

http://www.cnn.com/2015/07/29/politics/trump-breast-pump-statement/

http://www.cnn.com/2015/08/07/politics/
donald-trump-rosie-odonnell-feud/

http://www.cnn.com/2016/05/09/politics/
axe-files-axelrod-anderson-cooper/

http://www.cnn.com/2016/05/11/opinions/
donald-trump-support-mcenany/?iid=ob_article_footer_expansion

http://www.hollywoodreporter.com/gallery/
donald-trump-his-20-best-432843/1-vs-bill-maher

http://www.huffingtonpost.com/entry/
trump-megyn-kelly-debate-fox-news_us_55c5f6b3e4b0f73b20b989a7

http://www.huffingtonpost.com/sikivu-hutchinson/straight-outta-rape-
cultu_b_7942554.html

http://www.iwpr.org/initiatives/pay-equity-and-discrimination

http://www.nationalreview.com/article/430081/
she-threatened-me-juanita-broaddrick-hillarys-role-covering-bill-clinton

http://www.nytimes.com/2014/09/21/magazine/how-gary-harts-downfall-
forever-changed-american-politics.html?_r=0&version=meter+at+3&modu
le=meter-Links&pgtype=article&contentId=&mediaId=&referrer=https%
3A%2F%2Fwww.google.com&priority=true&action=click&contentCollec
tion=meter-links-click

http://www.politico.com/story/2015/05/

hillary-clinton-rappers-50-cent-support-118177

http://www.slate.com/articles/news_and_politics/cover_story/2016/07/
the_people_who_hate_hillary_clinton_the_most.html

http://www.xxlmag.com/news/2016/04/rappers-endorsing-hillary-clinton/

https://www.erictrumpfoundation.com/board-of-directors/lynne-m.-

https://www.washingtonpost.com/news/the-fix/wp/2015/08/08/
so-which-women-has-donald-trump-called-dogs-and-fat-pigs/

https://www.washingtonpost.com/politics/donald-trump-a-champion-of-
women-his-female-employees-think-so/2015/11/23/7eafac80-88da-11e5-
9a07-453018f9a0ec_story.html

CHAPTER 3

Painter, Nell Irvin. *The History of White People*. New York: W.W. Norton,
2010.

http://blackamericaweb.com/2016/07/24/donald-trump-is-full-of-it/

http://everydayfeminism.com/2015/11/lessons-white-privilege-poc/

http://www.heritage.org/research/testimony/2015/building-an-
opportunity-economy-the-state-of-small-business-and-entrepreneurship

http://hollywoodlife.com/2016/06/09/
valedictorian-illegal-immigrant-tx-graduation-speech-larissa-martinez/

http://mediamatters.org/video/2016/03/17/
bill-oreilly-trump-is-not-a-racist/209384

http://www.nationalreview.com/article/420321/
democratic-party-racist-history-mona-charen

http://www.nationalreview.com/article/432679/
donald-trump-melania-trump-immigration-h1b-visa

http://www.nationalreview.com/article/432876/donald-trump-white-working-class-dysfunction-real-opportunity-needed-not-trump

http://www.nationalreview.com/g-file/434455/donald-trump-white-working-class-what-trumps-defenders-get-wrong

http://www.nytimes.com/2015/09/23/nyregion/race-and-class-collide-in-a-plan-for-two-brooklyn-schools.html

http://www.nytimes.com/2016/07/14/us/politics/donald-trump-white-identity.html

http://www.politico.com/blogs/new-hampshire-primary-2016-live-updates/2016/02/donald-trump-2016-election-rich-people-218940

http://www.realclearpolitics.com/articles/2016/06/21/trumps_attack_on_freedom_of_religion_130942.html

http://www.theatlantic.com/politics/archive/2015/12/donald-trumps-call-to-ban-muslim-immigrants/419298/

http://www.theatlantic.com/politics/archive/2016/03/who-are-donald-trumps-supporters-really/471714/

http://www.wnd.com/2016/07/why-trump-has-so-little-of-african-american-vote/

http://www.wnyc.org/story/race-and-dating-navigating-love-and-white-privilege/

http://www.zerohedge.com/news/2016-06-10/donald-trump-voter-went-see-him-speak-protesters-broke-his-nose?page=2

https://www.washingtonpost.com/news/the-fix/wp/2016/02/26/why-hillary-clintons-super-predator-apology-is-such-a-big-moment-for-political-protest/

https://www.washingtonpost.com/news/the-fix/wp/2016/08/29/could-donald-trumps-border-wall-really-just-be-a-virtual-wall-not-according-to-trump

https://www.washingtonpost.com/news/wonk/wp/2015/02/12/the-fbi-director-just-quoted-from-avenue-qs-everyones-a-little-bit-racist-thats-huge/

https://www.washingtonpost.com/opinions/i-hate-donald-trump-but-he-might-get-my-vote/2016/06/28/ddeee5f8-398d-11e6-9ccd-d6005beac8b3_story.html?utm_term=.957418273dc2

https://www.washingtonpost.com/politics/inside-the-governments-racial-bias-case-against-donald-trumps-company-and-how-he-fought-it/2016/01/23/fb90163e-bfbe-11e5-bcda-62a36b394160_story.html

CHAPTER 4

"Can She Fix It." *The Economist*. Apr 23, 2016

"Poor Donald." *The Economist*. Jun 25, 2016.

Scrubs. "My Brother, My Keeper." Season 2, Episode 14. 2003.

Von Drehle, David. "Destination Unknown." *Time Magazine*. Mar 14, 2016.

http://abcnews.go.com/Politics/dem-vp-candidate-tim-kaine-heads-church-sings/story?id=40837086

http://articles.chicagotribune.com/1998-12-18/news/9812180366_1_impeachment-house-speaker-elect-bob-livingston-monica-lewinsky

http://lawnewz.com/high-profile/bill-clinton-should-know-better-than-to-meet-with-the-attorney-general-amid-email-investigation/

http://lawnewz.com/high-profile/man-admits-to-role-in-funneling-foreign-donations-to-obama-campaign/

http://reason.com/blog/2016/07/23/glenn-beck-im-probably-going-to-vote-for

http://theweek.com/speedreads/631424/clinton-reportedly-wants-hamilton-performance-democratic-convention

http://www.cnn.com/2011/POLITICS/04/29/politicians.swear.list/

http://www.cnn.com/2016/01/27/politics/
donald-trump-voters-2016-election/

http://www.elpasoproud.com/news/local/el-paso-news/
dnc-chief-debbie-wasserman-schultz-stepping-aside-after-convention

http://www.jta.org/1988/07/20/archive/
orthodox-child-with-rare-ailment-is-rescued-aboard-tycoons-jet

http://www.livestrong.com/
article/355384-why-is-football-the-most-popular-sport-in-america/

http://www.mcclatchydc.com/news/politics-government/election/
article85883852.html

http://www.nationalreview.com/article/434431/
donald-trumps-presidential-maturation-myth

http://www.nationalreview.com/article/434916/ted-cruz-why-he-lost

http://www.ontheissues.org/Economic/Tim_Kaine_Budget_+_Economy.htm

http://www.politico.com/magazine/story/2015/08/
the-absolute-trumpest-121328

http://www.realclearpolitics.com/articles/2016/06/21/trump_evangelicals_
seek_common_cause_130960.html

http://www.theblaze.com/stories/2016/07/28/
dnc-hack-gets-bigger-as-wikileaks-releases-staff-voicemails/

http://www.thesportsnotebook.
com/2014/01/2007-new-york-giants-sports-history-articles/

http://www.va.gov/vetdata/docs/SpecialReports/State_Summaries_
Colorado.pdf

https://www2.census.gov/library/visualizations/2015/comm/vets/co-vet.pdf

https://ballotpedia.org/

Changes_in_Net_Worth_of_U.S._Senators_and_Representatives_
(Personal_Gain_Index)

https://cdn.ampproject.org/c/s/www.washingtonpost.com/amphtml/
politics/clinton-and-allies-open-new-front-against-trump-his-profits-from-
the-housing-crash/2016/05/24/16399474-21f3-11e6-8690-f14ca9de2972_
story.html

https://www.entrepreneur.com/article/248450

https://www.psychologytoday.com/blog/
what-mentally-strong-people-dont-do/201511/7-things-only-narcissists-do

https://www.youtube.com/watch?v=xgQ14DqbC-g

CHAPTER 5

"Fear trumps hope." *The Economist*. May 7, 2016.

Meacham, Jon. "What A President Needs To Know." *Time Magazine*. Jul 25, 2016.

http://extras.denverpost.com/aurora-va-hospital/

http://extras.denverpost.com/veterans/

http://smallbusiness.chron.com/become-successful-real-estate-
developer-22502.html

http://thefederalist.com/2014/01/17/the-death-of-expertise/

http://time.com/4443382/
donald-trump-economic-speech-detroit-transcript/

http://www.alternet.org/election-2016/6-most-meaningless-words-
politicians-and-pundits-throw-around-and-should-be-abandoned

http://www.bbc.com/news/magazine-26384712

http://www.britannica.com/biography/Donald-Trump

http://www.economicpolicyjournal.com/2016/07/trump-threatens-to-pull-us-out-of-world.html

http://www.forbes.com/sites/karstenstrauss/2016/03/02/11-most-famous-career-changes/#11ab810e4abe

http://www.nationalreview.com/article/434436/donald-trumps-transgender-bathroom-abortion-harriet-tubman-positions-all-wrong

http://www.npr.org/2015/06/09/413178870/the-unfinished-va-hospital-thats-more-than-1-billion-over-budget

http://www.npr.org/2016/08/18/490558406/watch-donald-trump-expresses-regret-for-sometimes-saying-the-wrong-thing

http://www.nytimes.com/2015/12/13/opinion/campaign-stops/all-politicians-lie-some-lie-more-than-others.html?_r=0

http://www.nytimes.com/interactive/2016/08/08/us/politics/national-security-letter-trump.html?_r=0

http://www.realclearpolitics.com/video/2016/06/21/hillary_clinton_warns_of_a_trump_recession.html

http://www.usgovernmentspending.com/percent_gdp

http://zidilife.com/far-go/

https://www.washingtonpost.com/opinions/the-biggest-threat-to-the-us-economy/2016/06/20/af1f0120-371e-11e6-8f7c-d4c723a2becb_story.html?utm_term=.2c047a7bf679

CHAPTER 6

http://foreignpolicy.com/2015/10/27/donald-trump-is-right-about-foreign-policy/

http://www.nytimes.com/2015/04/24/us/cash-flowed-to-clinton-foundation-as-russians-pressed-for-control-of-uranium-company.html

http://www.pbs.org/wgbh/americanexperience/features/general-article/
fdr-foreign/

http://www.politico.com/magazine/story/2016/01/
donald-trump-foreign-policy-213546

http://www.redstate.com/setonmotley/2016/06/27/
coming-soon-internet-speed-government/

http://www.usatoday.com/story/money/business/2013/04/09/
coffee-mania/2069335/

https://www.buzzfeed.com/ilanbenmeir/that-time-trump-spent-nearly-
100000-on-an-ad-criticizing-us?utm_term=.ntO0rDZYV#.kqNZaQRg5

CHAPTER 7

http://www.adl.org/assets/pdf/education-outreach/what-is-the-dream-act-
and-who-are-the-dreamers.pdf

http://www.civilrights.org/resources/civilrights101/chronology.html

http://www.ijreview.com/2015/11/461306-these-5-acts-of-kindness-
reveal-theres-more-to-donald-trump-than-just-his-celebrity-persona/

http://www.msnbc.com/msnbc/
the-art-the-flip-flop-breaking-down-the-2016-reversals

http://www.nytimes.com/1988/03/01/opinion/in-the-nation-a-case-for-
flip-flops.html

http://www.politico.com/story/2015/08/
donald-trump-2016-why-is-he-running-121553

http://www.slate.com/articles/news_and_politics/politics/2015/05/
america_s_best_presidents_have_been_flip_floppers_scott_walker_and_
hillary.html

https://en.wikipedia.org/wiki/Flip-flop_(politics)

https://www.washingtonpost.com/opinions/nixons-great-decision-on-china-40-years-later/2012/02/10/gIQAtFh34Q_story.html

https://www.washingtonpost.com/posteverything/wp/2016/05/10/why-donald-trump-seems-invulnerable-to-the-flip-flop-charge/

CHAPTER 8

http://fundersandfounders.com/how-steve-jobs-started/

http://thinkprogress.org/politics/2016/03/04/3756135/trump-steaks-a-definitive-history/

http://us-presidents.insidegov.com/q/16/9699/What-were-President-Theodore-Roosevelt-s-accomplishments

http://www.businessinsider.com/how-donald-trump-got-rich-2016-3

http://www.businessinsider.com/steve-wynn-explains-why-atlantic-city-is-obsolete-2014-7

http://www.cardplayer.com/poker-news/20743-revel-owner-might-abandon-reopening-plans-says-new-jersey-just-stinks

http://www.forbes.com/sites/realspin/2015/12/15/donald-trump-teddy-roosevelt/#7ad3537349cc

http://www.internationalbusinessguide.org/trump-business-career/

http://www.investopedia.com/university/steve-jobs-biography/steve-jobs-success-story.asp

CHAPTER 9

"The Brawl Begins." *The Economist.* Jan 30, 2016.

"When Harry Met Donald." *Time Magazine.* Jul 25, 2016.

Miller, Zeke J. "A Tale of Three Headquarters." *Time Magazine.* Jun 6, 2016.

Trump, Donald, and Tony Schwartz. *Trump: The Art of the Deal.* New York: Random House, 1988.

Trump, Donald. *Crippled America: How to Make America Great Again.* New York: Threshold Editions, 2015.

Williamson, Kevin and Charles C.W. Cooke. *Mad Dogs & Englishmen.* Podcast Audio, August 2015 - August 1 2016.

https://ricochet.com/series/mad-dogs-englishmen/.

http://patriotpost.us/alexander/41195

http://reason.com/blog/2016/07/22/
donald-trumps-speech-at-the-rnc-last-nig

http://usconservatives.about.com/od/glossaryterms/g/The-Establishment-Definition-Of-The-Republican-Establishment.htm

http://www.bloomberg.com/politics/articles/2016-06-29/
clinton-s-private-e-mail-use-said-to-frustrate-top-aide-huma-abedin

http://www.commondreams.org/news/2016/07/23/establishment-wins-again-dnc-rules-committee-rejects-proposal-abolish-superdelegates

http://www.foxnews.com/politics/2016/08/08/revolt-on-right-commentators-bash-trump-in-psychiatric-terms.html

http://www.nationalreview.com/article/422347/
trump-virus-and-its-symptoms-charles-c-w-cooke

http://www.newyorker.com/news/news-desk/
how-the-republican-establishment-lost-to-trump-on-russia

http://www.nytimes.com/2016/02/17/opinion/campaign-stops/donald-trumps-secret-channelling-andrew-jackson.html?_r=0

http://www.nytimes.com/2016/03/30/opinion/campaign-stops/who-are-the-angriest-republicans.html?_r=0

http://www.politico.com/story/2016/07/

off-message-transcript-ted-cruz-225655

http://www.realclearpolitics.com/articles/2016/06/22/why_potential_
trump_donors_arent_stepping_up_130965.html

http://www.rushlimbaugh.com/daily/2016/08/08/
who_would_believe_trump_hates_babies

http://www.theatlantic.com/politics/archive/2016/05/a-dialogue-with-a-
22-year-old-donald-trump-supporter/484232/

https://fairtax-structure-psyclone.netdna-ssl.com/client_assets/fairtaxorg/
media/attachments/56c4/b27f/6970/2d56/0841/0000/56c4b27f697
02d5608410000.pdf?1455731327

https://www.project-syndicate.org/commentary/
why-democracy-requires-experts-by-jean-pisani-ferry-2016-08

https://www.washingtonpost.com/politics/inside-the-democratic-
partys-scramble-for-big-money/2016/07/24/0f02b56c-51c0-11e6-b7de-
dfe509430c39_story.html

MISCELLANEOUS

"NCLB Gets Left Behind." *The Economist.* Dec 12, 2015.

http://dailycaller.com/2016/07/24/leaked-dnc-documents-show-plans-to-
reward-big-donors-with-federal-appointments/

http://reason.com/archives/2016/06/21/why-hillary-hates-uber

http://usuncut.com/politics/dnc-leaks-9-emails/

http://www.businessinsider.com/
reid-rips-gop-leaders-in-blistering-statement-2016-7

http://www.valleynewslive.com/content/news/Disturbing-DNC-email-
calls-Hispanic-outreach-taco-bowl-engagement-388081582.html

https://www.facebook.com/note.php?note_id=10150516734848435

https://www.nraila.org/articles/20151009/clinton-says-that-the-second-amendment-does-not-protect-an-individual-right-to-keep-and-bear-arms

https://www.nraila.org/articles/20151016/hillary-clinton-supports-australia-style-gun-confiscation

https://www.washingtonpost.com/investigations/capitol-assets-congresss-wealthiest-mostly-shielded-in-deep-recession/2012/10/06/5a70605c-102f-11e2-acc1-e927767f41cd_story.html

https://www.washingtonpost.com/news/the-fix/wp/2016/07/18/gop-convention-begins-with-tears-and-the-strongest-possible-indictment-of-hillary-clinton/

CPSIA information can be obtained
at www.ICGtesting.com
Printed in the USA
LVHW021531070521
686793LV00029B/1298